Mastering Productivity: Proven Strategies to Stay Focused and Achieve Your Goals

Table of Contents

1. **Introduction**
   - Why Productivity Matters
   - The Productivity Myths
   - How to Use This Book

2. **Chapter 1: Understanding Productivity**
   - The Science of Productivity
   - Productivity vs. Busyness
   - Common Productivity Pitfalls

3. **Chapter 2: Setting Goals and Priorities**
   - SMART Goals Framework
   - Prioritization Techniques
   - Balancing Short-Term and Long-Term Goals

4. **Chapter 3: Time Management Strategies**
   - The Pomodoro Technique
   - Time Blocking and Scheduling
   - Overcoming Procrastination

5. **Chapter 4: Tools and Techniques**

- Productivity Apps and Software
   - Task Management Systems
   - The Power of Checklists

6. **Chapter 5: Habits and Routines**
   - Building Productive Habits
   - Morning and Evening Routines
   - The Role of Discipline and Consistency

7. **Chapter 6: Overcoming Challenges**
   - Dealing with Burnout
   - Staying Motivated
   - Managing Distractions and Interruptions

8. **Chapter 7: Productivity in Different Contexts**
   - Productivity at Work
   - Managing Home and Personal Life
   - Remote Work Productivity

9. **Chapter 8: Continuous Improvement**
   - Reviewing and Reflecting on Your Progress
   - Adapting and Evolving Your Strategies
   - Lifelong Learning and Growth

10. **Conclusion**
    - Recap of Key Points
    - Your Roadmap to Mastery
    - Final Thoughts

11. **Resources**
    - Recommended Books and Articles
    - Productivity Tools and Apps
    - Online Communities and Support

Introduction

Why Productivity Matters

In today's fast-paced world, productivity has become a buzzword. Everyone from CEOs to students is constantly seeking ways to be more productive. But what does productivity really mean, and why does it matter so much?

At its core, productivity is about getting things done efficiently. It's the measure of how effectively you can accomplish tasks, whether at work, in your personal life, or in any other area where you have goals. But productivity isn't just about checking items off a to-do list; it's about achieving meaningful progress towards your goals. When you're truly productive, you're not just busy—you're making real, tangible progress.

The Impact of Productivity on Success

Productivity is directly linked to success. Whether you're aiming for career advancement, personal growth, or simply managing day-to-day responsibilities, being productive allows you to reach your objectives faster and with less stress. Think about it: the more productive you are, the more you can achieve in less time. This efficiency frees up time for other pursuits, whether it's spending time with family, pursuing hobbies, or even taking care of your well-being.

Successful people aren't just lucky—they've mastered the art of productivity. They know how to focus their energy on what truly matters, eliminate distractions, and use their time wisely. By being productive, you're essentially building the foundation for your future success.

Reducing Stress and Overwhelm

Another reason productivity matters is its impact on your mental health. When you're productive, you're less likely to feel overwhelmed by tasks piling up. Instead of feeling like you're constantly playing catch-up, you'll experience a sense of control over your time and workload. This sense of control reduces stress and boosts your overall well-being.

Consider how it feels when you've had a productive day—you're more relaxed, satisfied, and ready to unwind. On the other hand, when you've been unproductive, you might feel anxious, guilty, or stressed about the tasks left undone. By improving your productivity, you can create a more balanced and stress-free life.

Maximizing Your Potential

Productivity isn't just about getting more done—it's about getting the right things done. It's about maximizing your potential and making the most of your time and talents. Each of us has a unique set of skills and abilities, and by being productive, we can channel these strengths into meaningful achievements.

When you focus on productivity, you're not just working harder; you're working smarter. You're identifying the tasks that will have the most significant impact and dedicating your energy to those tasks. This approach allows you to make the most of your time and ensures that you're moving closer to your long-term goals every day.

Living a Fulfilling Life

Ultimately, productivity matters because it contributes to a fulfilling life. When you're productive, you have the time and energy to pursue your passions, maintain strong relationships, and take care of yourself. You're able to create a life that aligns with your values and aspirations.

By mastering productivity, you're not just achieving more—you're building a life filled with purpose, satisfaction, and balance. In the end, that's what true productivity is all about: living a life that you love and are proud of.

Conclusion

Productivity is more than just a tool for getting things done—it's a pathway to success, reduced stress, and a fulfilling life. By understanding why productivity matters, you can start making small changes today that will lead to big results tomorrow.

The Productivity Myths

In the quest to become more productive, many of us fall victim to common myths that can actually hinder our progress. These misconceptions are often deeply ingrained, leading us to adopt habits and mindsets that do more harm than good. Let's take a closer look at some of these productivity myths and debunk them, so you can focus on what truly works.

Myth 1: Being Busy Equals Being Productive

One of the most prevalent myths is that being busy means you're being productive. We often equate a full schedule with success, believing that the more tasks we're juggling, the more productive we must be. However, being busy doesn't necessarily mean you're getting important things done.

Productivity is about effectiveness, not just activity. It's about focusing on tasks that move you closer to your goals, rather than just filling your day with work. You could be busy all day but accomplish little if you're not focusing on the right things. To truly be productive, prioritize tasks that have the most impact, and don't be afraid to say no to less important activities.

Myth 2: Multitasking Boosts Productivity

Many people believe that multitasking is a key to getting more done. The idea is that by handling multiple tasks at once, you can be more efficient. However, research shows that multitasking actually reduces productivity.

When you try to do multiple things simultaneously, your brain has to switch back and forth between tasks, which can slow you down and lead to mistakes. Instead of multitasking, focus on one task at a time. This approach, known as single-tasking, allows you to give your full attention to the task at hand, leading to higher quality work and faster completion times.

Myth 3: You Need to Work Long Hours to Be Productive

There's a common belief that working long hours is the only way to be truly productive. This myth is rooted in the idea that more time spent working equals more output. However, working excessively long hours can actually be counterproductive.

When you push yourself to work too long without adequate breaks, you're likely to experience burnout, fatigue, and a decline in the quality of your work. True productivity isn't about the number of hours you work, but how effectively you use those hours. Focus on working smarter, not harder, by setting clear boundaries, taking regular breaks, and ensuring you have time to recharge.

Myth 4: Productivity Is About Willpower and Motivation

Another common myth is that productivity is all about willpower and staying motivated. While motivation can help, it's not always reliable. Willpower tends to fluctuate, and there will be days when you just don't feel motivated to work.

The key to consistent productivity isn't relying solely on motivation; it's about building systems and habits that support your goals. This means creating routines, setting up your environment for success, and using tools and techniques that help you stay on track even when motivation is low. By focusing on habits rather than willpower, you can maintain productivity over the long term.

Myth 5: There's a Perfect Productivity System

Many people search for the perfect productivity system, believing that if they find the right one, it will solve all their problems. The truth is, there's no one-size-fits-all solution when it comes to productivity. What works for one person might not work for another, and that's okay.

The key is to experiment with different tools, techniques, and strategies until you find what works best for you. Productivity is a personal journey, and it's important to tailor your approach to fit your unique needs, goals, and lifestyle. Don't be discouraged if one system doesn't work—keep experimenting until you find the right fit.

Conclusion

By understanding and debunking these common productivity myths, you can avoid falling into traps that waste your time and energy. Remember, true productivity is about focusing on what matters, working smart, and creating systems that support your success. Once you let go of these myths, you'll be on your way to achieving more with less effort.

How to Use This Book

Congratulations on taking the first step toward mastering productivity! This book is designed to be your guide, helping you unlock your full potential and achieve your goals with greater ease and efficiency. Whether you're a busy professional, a student, or someone looking to bring more balance into your life, this book will provide you with the tools and strategies you need to be more productive. Here's how to make the most of it.

A Roadmap to Productivity

This book is structured to take you on a journey from understanding the fundamentals of productivity to implementing advanced strategies that can transform your life. Each chapter builds on the previous one, offering a comprehensive approach that covers all aspects of productivity—from goal setting and time management to overcoming challenges and maintaining balance.

While the chapters are designed to be read sequentially, you don't have to follow a strict order. If there's a particular area of productivity that you're struggling with, feel free to jump to that chapter and start there. The book is organized to be flexible, allowing you to tailor your reading experience to your specific needs.

Practical, Actionable Advice

One of the key features of this book is its focus on practicality. Productivity isn't just about theory; it's about applying what you learn to your daily life. Throughout the book, you'll find actionable tips, exercises, and real-world examples that you can implement right away.

To get the most out of this book, it's important to not just read passively but to engage with the material. When you come across an exercise or a tip that resonates with you, take a moment to try it out. Reflect on how it can be applied to your life and make adjustments as needed. The more you practice, the more these productivity strategies will become second nature.

Reflection and Growth

As you work through this book, you'll be encouraged to reflect on your progress and make adjustments along the way. Productivity is a continuous process, and what works for you today might need tweaking tomorrow. Each chapter includes prompts and questions designed to help you think critically about your habits, challenges, and successes.

Take time to answer these questions honestly. Use them as opportunities for self-discovery and growth. By regularly reflecting on your progress, you'll gain deeper insights into what drives your productivity and how you can improve over time.

Customizing Your Productivity Approach

One of the biggest myths about productivity is that there's a one-size-fits-all solution. This book recognizes that everyone's journey is different. What works for one person may not work for another, and that's perfectly fine. The strategies and techniques outlined in this book are meant to be customized to suit your unique needs and circumstances.

As you read, experiment with different approaches and see what resonates with you. If a particular technique doesn't work, don't be discouraged—try another one. The key is to find what fits your lifestyle and goals. Over time, you'll develop a personalized productivity system that works best for you.

Ongoing Support and Resources

Productivity isn't something you master overnight; it's a skill that develops over time. To support your ongoing journey, this book includes a Resources section at the end, packed with recommendations for further reading, productivity tools, and online communities. These resources are there to help you continue learning and growing long after you've finished the book.

If you ever find yourself struggling or in need of inspiration, revisit these resources or re-read specific chapters. Productivity is a dynamic process, and it's normal to need reminders and refreshers along the way.

Conclusion: Your Productivity Journey

This book is more than just a collection of tips and tricks—it's a guide to transforming the way you approach your time, tasks, and goals. By using this book actively and engaging with the material, you're setting yourself up for success. Remember, productivity isn't about perfection; it's about progress. Take what you learn, apply it to your life, and watch as you begin to achieve more with less stress and effort. Your journey to mastering productivity starts now.

Chapter 1: Understanding Productivity

The Science of Productivity

Productivity isn't just about working harder; it's about working smarter. But what does that really mean? At its core, productivity is deeply rooted in science—specifically, how our brains function, how we process information, and how we manage our time and energy. Understanding the science behind productivity can help you optimize your habits, make better decisions, and ultimately achieve more with less effort. Let's dive into some of the key scientific principles that underpin productivity.

The Role of the Brain

Your brain is the engine driving your productivity. However, it has limitations, and understanding these can help you work more effectively. One of the brain's key functions related to productivity is its ability to focus. Focus is controlled by the prefrontal cortex, which is responsible for decision-making, problem-solving, and attention.

However, the prefrontal cortex can only focus intensely for a limited period—typically around 90 minutes—before it starts to tire. This is why working in short bursts, followed by breaks, is far more effective than trying to work non-stop for hours. The Pomodoro Technique, for example, leverages this by encouraging people to work for 25 minutes and then take a 5-minute break. This approach aligns with the brain's natural rhythm, keeping it fresh and focused.

The Myth of Multitasking

Many people believe that multitasking is a sign of productivity. However, science tells us otherwise. The human brain isn't wired to handle multiple tasks at the same time effectively. When you try to multitask, what you're really doing is rapidly switching your attention between tasks, which significantly reduces your efficiency.

Studies have shown that multitasking can actually decrease productivity by up to 40%. This is because each time you switch tasks, your brain needs to reorient itself, which takes time and energy. Instead, focusing on one task at a time—also known as single-tasking—allows you to complete tasks more quickly and with better results.

The Power of Habits

Another critical aspect of productivity is the role of habits. According to research, around 40% of our daily actions are habits—automatic behaviors that we perform without much conscious thought. This is significant because habits free up mental energy for more complex tasks.

Building productive habits means setting up routines that support your goals. For example, if you make it a habit to plan your day each morning, you'll spend less time throughout the day deciding what to do next. The key to building habits is consistency. It takes an average of 66 days to form a new habit, so start small and stay committed.

Energy Management

While time management is often emphasized in productivity discussions, energy management is just as crucial. Your energy levels fluctuate throughout the day, influenced by factors like sleep, nutrition, and stress levels. The science of ultradian rhythms explains that our energy cycles in waves throughout the day, with peaks and troughs approximately every 90 minutes.

To maximize productivity, align your most challenging tasks with your energy peaks. For example, if you're most alert in the morning, tackle your most important work then. During low-energy periods, focus on less demanding tasks, or take a break to recharge.

The Importance of Sleep

Sleep is one of the most underrated factors in productivity. Scientific studies consistently show that sleep is critical for cognitive function, memory consolidation, and decision-making. When you're sleep-deprived, your ability to focus, solve problems, and manage your emotions is severely compromised.

Prioritizing quality sleep—ideally 7-9 hours per night—can significantly boost your productivity. Sleep helps your brain process information from the day, repair itself, and prepare for the next day's challenges. Consider creating a bedtime routine that helps you wind down, ensuring you get the rest you need to perform at your best.

The Science of Flow

Finally, one of the most powerful states for productivity is known as "flow." Flow is a mental state where you're fully immersed in a task, losing track of time and producing your best work. Psychologist Mihaly Csikszentmihalyi, who coined the term, found that flow occurs when you're working on a task that's challenging yet within your skill set.

Achieving flow regularly can lead to heightened creativity, greater satisfaction, and enhanced productivity. To get into flow, minimize distractions, set clear goals, and choose tasks that stretch your abilities without overwhelming you.

Conclusion

Productivity is not just a matter of working longer or harder—it's about understanding and leveraging the science behind how our brains and bodies work. By focusing on single-tasking, building productive habits, managing your energy, prioritizing sleep, and tapping into the flow state, you can optimize your productivity in a way that feels both natural and sustainable. With this scientific foundation, you're well-equipped to make the most of your time and achieve your goals more effectively.

Productivity vs. Busyness

In our fast-paced world, it's easy to equate busyness with productivity. We often wear our packed schedules like badges of honor, believing that the more tasks we juggle, the more accomplished we must be. But here's the truth: being busy and being productive are not the same. In fact, confusing the two can lead to burnout, frustration, and a lack of real progress toward your goals. Let's explore the critical differences between productivity and busyness and why it's essential to focus on the former rather than the latter.

The Illusion of Busyness

Busyness is often about appearances. It's that feeling of being constantly in motion, with endless tasks, meetings, and deadlines. Many people pride themselves on being busy, believing it's a sign of importance or effectiveness. But busyness can be deceptive. Just because your day is full doesn't mean you're making meaningful progress.

Busyness often involves low-impact activities—tasks that may feel urgent but don't contribute significantly to your long-term goals. It's easy to fill your time with such activities, whether it's answering emails, attending meetings, or dealing with minor issues that could be delegated or postponed. While these tasks might keep you occupied, they often don't move the needle when it comes to real achievement.

What Is True Productivity?

Productivity, on the other hand, is about effectiveness. It's not about how much you do, but about how much you accomplish that truly matters. Being productive means focusing on high-impact activities—those that align with your goals and bring you closer to achieving them. It's about working smarter, not harder.

When you're productive, you prioritize tasks based on their importance and impact. You're intentional about how you spend your time, making sure that your efforts are directed toward activities that yield the most significant results. Productivity isn't about cramming as much as possible into your day; it's about making the best use of your time and energy to achieve meaningful outcomes.

The Pitfalls of Busyness

One of the biggest dangers of busyness is that it can lead to burnout. When you're constantly busy, you may feel overwhelmed, stressed, and exhausted. You might also find yourself stuck in a cycle of reactive work, always responding to the next urgent task without ever having the time to focus on what's truly important.

Busyness can also lead to a lack of fulfillment. When you're focused solely on getting through your to-do list, you might miss out on the satisfaction that comes from making real progress toward your goals. Instead of feeling accomplished, you might feel like you're spinning your wheels, working hard but not really getting anywhere.

How to Shift from Busyness to Productivity

Making the shift from busyness to productivity requires a change in mindset and approach. Here are some strategies to help you focus on what truly matters:

1. **Prioritize Your Tasks:** Start by identifying the tasks that have the most significant impact on your goals. Use tools like the Eisenhower Matrix to categorize tasks into four quadrants: urgent and important, important but not urgent, urgent but not important, and neither urgent nor important. Focus on tasks that fall into the important categories, and try to minimize time spent on the others.

2. **Practice Single-Tasking:** Instead of trying to multitask, which can dilute your focus and reduce efficiency, commit to single-tasking. Give your full attention to one task at a time, and complete it before moving on to the next. This approach leads to higher quality work and greater satisfaction.

3. **Set Clear Goals:** Productivity is driven by clear, specific goals. When you know exactly what you want to achieve, it's easier to focus on the tasks that will get you there. Break down your goals into actionable steps, and prioritize those steps in your daily work.

4. **Learn to Say No:** Part of being productive is protecting your time. Learn to say no to tasks, meetings, or commitments that don't align with your goals or add value to your work. It's okay to set boundaries and prioritize your most important work.

5. **Reflect and Adjust:** Regularly review your progress and reflect on how you're spending your time. Are you focusing on high-impact activities, or are you getting caught up in busyness? Use these reflections to make adjustments and ensure you're staying on the path to true productivity.

Conclusion: Choose Impact Over Activity

In the end, the difference between productivity and busyness comes down to impact. Being busy might make you feel like you're accomplishing a lot, but if your efforts aren't moving you closer to your goals, that busyness is ultimately unproductive. True productivity is about making the most of your time and energy, focusing on what truly matters, and achieving meaningful results. By shifting your focus from activity to impact, you can work smarter, achieve more, and find greater fulfillment in your work and life.

Common Productivity Pitfalls

When it comes to productivity, even the most well-intentioned efforts can sometimes lead us astray. We all strive to be more efficient and effective, but it's easy to fall into traps that diminish our progress instead of enhancing it. Understanding these common productivity pitfalls can help you avoid them and stay on the path to achieving your goals.

Pitfall 1: Overcommitting and Multitasking

One of the most prevalent productivity pitfalls is overcommitting. It's tempting to say "yes" to every request, project, or opportunity that comes your way, especially if you're eager to prove yourself or fear missing out. However, spreading yourself too thin can lead to burnout and diminish the quality of your work.

Closely related to overcommitting is the habit of multitasking. Many people believe that handling multiple tasks at once will help them get more done, but in reality, it often leads to mistakes and reduced efficiency. Research shows that the human brain isn't designed to focus on more than one task at a time. When you switch between tasks, your brain needs time to refocus, which can slow you down and lead to errors.

Solution: Learn to set boundaries and prioritize your commitments. It's okay to say no to tasks that don't align with your goals or aren't essential. Focus on single-tasking—giving your full attention to one task at a time. You'll find that you complete tasks more quickly and with better results when you're not constantly dividing your focus.

Pitfall 2: Procrastination and Perfectionism

Procrastination is another common pitfall that can derail productivity. It's easy to put off tasks, especially those that seem daunting or unpleasant. However, delaying work only leads to increased stress and often results in rushed, subpar output.

Perfectionism often goes hand in hand with procrastination. The desire to do everything perfectly can be paralyzing, causing you to spend excessive time on minor details or avoiding starting a task altogether.

This can lead to missed deadlines and a lack of progress on important goals.

Solution: Combat procrastination by breaking tasks into smaller, manageable steps. Start with the easiest or most enjoyable part of a task to build momentum. For perfectionism, remind yourself that done is better than perfect. Set a reasonable standard for your work, and recognize that striving for perfection can sometimes prevent you from completing anything at all.

Pitfall 3: Lack of Clear Goals and Prioritization

Without clear goals, it's easy to drift through your day without a sense of direction. When you don't know what you're working towards, you might end up focusing on tasks that are urgent but not important, rather than those that will bring you closer to your long-term objectives.

Failing to prioritize is another major pitfall. Even if you have clear goals, if you don't prioritize your tasks effectively, you might spend your time on less critical activities, leaving the most important work undone.

Solution: Set clear, specific goals that align with your broader objectives. Break these goals down into actionable tasks, and prioritize them based on their importance and impact. Tools like the Eisenhower Matrix can help you distinguish between tasks that are urgent and important, and those that can be delegated or postponed.

Pitfall 4: Inefficient Time Management

Time management is at the heart of productivity, but many people struggle with it. Poor time management can manifest in various ways, such as failing to allocate sufficient time for important tasks, underestimating how long tasks will take, or neglecting to schedule breaks.

Another common issue is the inability to manage distractions. Whether it's constant notifications, interruptions from colleagues, or the temptation to check social media, distractions can eat away at your time and focus.

Solution: Develop a time management system that works for you, whether it's time-blocking, using a planner, or adopting the Pomodoro Technique. Be realistic about how long tasks will take, and make sure to schedule breaks to avoid burnout. To manage distractions, set specific times to check email or social media, and create a workspace that minimizes interruptions.

Pitfall 5: Neglecting Self-Care

Finally, one of the most overlooked productivity pitfalls is neglecting self-care. Many people believe that being productive means working non-stop, but this approach can lead to exhaustion and decreased efficiency over time. When you're tired, stressed, or unhealthy, your ability to focus and perform at your best diminishes.

Solution: Prioritize self-care as part of your productivity strategy. This includes getting enough sleep, eating well, exercising regularly, and taking time to relax and recharge. Remember that productivity is not about working as much as possible; it's about working effectively and sustainably.

Conclusion: Avoiding the Traps

By recognizing and addressing these common productivity pitfalls, you can avoid unnecessary setbacks and make steady progress toward your goals. Remember, productivity isn't about perfection—it's about consistently making smart choices that help you achieve meaningful results. With awareness and proactive strategies, you can overcome these challenges and become more productive in a way that enhances both your work and your well-being.

Chapter 2: Setting Goals and Priorities

SMART Goals Framework

Setting goals is an essential part of achieving success, whether in your personal life, career, or any other area. However, not all goals are created equal. Some goals are vague and difficult to measure, making them hard to achieve. That's where the SMART Goals Framework comes in. SMART is an acronym that stands for Specific, Measurable, Achievable, Relevant, and Time-bound. This framework helps you set clear, attainable, and meaningful goals that increase your chances of success. Let's break down each component of SMART goals and how you can apply them to your life.

Specific: Be Clear and Precise

The first element of a SMART goal is that it must be specific. A specific goal answers the questions: What exactly do you want to achieve? Why is this goal important? Who is involved? Where will it take place? Which resources or constraints are involved?

For example, instead of setting a vague goal like "I want to get in shape," a specific goal would be, "I want to lose 10 pounds in three months by exercising four times a week and following a healthy diet." This goal clearly defines what you want to achieve, the method you'll use, and the timeframe in which you want to accomplish it. Specific goals eliminate ambiguity and provide a clear direction.

Measurable: Track Your Progress

The second component of SMART goals is measurability. A goal must be measurable so you can track your progress and stay motivated.

Measurable goals answer the question: How will I know when I have achieved this goal?

Continuing with the previous example, "losing 10 pounds" is a measurable goal because you can track your weight loss over time. You can measure your progress by stepping on the scale weekly, keeping a food diary, or tracking your workouts. Measurable goals allow you to see how far you've come and how much further you need to go, which helps you stay focused and motivated.

Achievable: Be Realistic and Challenging

A SMART goal must be achievable, meaning it should be realistic given your resources and constraints, yet still challenging. Achievable goals answer the question: Is this goal attainable with the resources I have?

While it's essential to set goals that push you out of your comfort zone, it's equally important to ensure they are within reach. Setting an unrealistic goal, like "losing 30 pounds in one month," is likely to lead to frustration and failure. Instead, focus on setting a goal that requires effort but is still possible, such as "losing 10 pounds in three months." Achievable goals help you stay committed because they strike the right balance between challenge and feasibility.

Relevant: Align with Your Values and Long-Term Objectives

The fourth component of a SMART goal is relevance. A relevant goal aligns with your broader life goals and values, ensuring that it matters to you and fits within your larger objectives. Relevant goals answer the question: Why is this goal important to me? Does it align with my long-term plans?

For instance, if your long-term objective is to lead a healthier lifestyle, losing weight and improving fitness levels is relevant. However, if the goal doesn't align with your values or isn't something you genuinely care about, it's unlikely to sustain your motivation. Setting relevant goals ensures that your efforts are directed toward something that truly matters to you, increasing the likelihood of success.

Time-bound: Set a Deadline

The final element of SMART goals is that they must be time-bound. This means setting a deadline by which you want to achieve your goal. Time-bound goals answer the question: When do I want to achieve this goal?

A time-bound goal creates a sense of urgency and helps you prioritize your actions. For example, "I want to lose 10 pounds in three months" provides a clear timeframe, making it easier to break down the goal into smaller, actionable steps, such as losing 3-4 pounds per month. Without a deadline, it's easy to procrastinate or lose focus, so setting a specific timeframe helps you stay on track.

Conclusion: The Power of SMART Goals

The SMART Goals Framework is a powerful tool that can help you set goals that are clear, actionable, and achievable. By ensuring your goals are specific, measurable, achievable, relevant, and time-bound, you're more likely to stay focused, motivated, and on track to achieving them. Whether you're aiming for personal growth, career advancement, or any other objective, applying the SMART framework can significantly increase your chances of success. Instead of vague aspirations, you'll have a well-defined roadmap that guides you toward your desired outcomes, making your goals not just dreams, but realities.

Prioritization Techniques

In a world where there's always too much to do and too little time, effective prioritization is key to staying productive and achieving your goals. Prioritization isn't just about deciding what to do first; it's about making sure that you're spending your time on the tasks that truly matter. Mastering prioritization techniques can help you manage your workload more efficiently, reduce stress, and ensure that your efforts are aligned with your most important objectives. Let's explore some of the most effective prioritization techniques that you can use to maximize your productivity.

1. The Eisenhower Matrix: Urgent vs. Important

One of the most popular prioritization techniques is the Eisenhower Matrix, also known as the Urgent-Important Matrix. This technique, popularized by former U.S. President Dwight D. Eisenhower, helps you categorize tasks based on their urgency and importance.

The Eisenhower Matrix divides tasks into four quadrants:
- **Quadrant 1: Urgent and Important** – These tasks require immediate attention and are crucial to your goals. Examples include meeting deadlines or handling emergencies. Focus on completing these tasks first.
- **Quadrant 2: Important but Not Urgent** – These are tasks that are key to long-term success but don't need to be done immediately, such as strategic planning or personal development. Schedule time to work on these tasks to prevent them from becoming urgent.
- **Quadrant 3: Urgent but Not Important** – These tasks demand immediate attention but don't significantly impact your long-term goals, like attending unnecessary meetings or responding to non-essential emails. Try to delegate or minimize these tasks.
- **Quadrant 4: Not Urgent and Not Important** – These tasks are distractions that don't contribute to your goals, such as mindless internet browsing or unnecessary social media use. Eliminate or limit these activities.

By using the Eisenhower Matrix, you can prioritize tasks that are both important and urgent, while also making time for tasks that are important but not yet urgent, ensuring you stay on track toward your goals.

2. The ABCDE Method: Simple and Effective

The ABCDE Method is a straightforward yet effective prioritization technique developed by time management expert Brian Tracy. It involves categorizing your tasks into five levels of priority, each assigned a letter:

- **A:** Must-do tasks that are essential and have serious consequences if not completed. These are your highest-priority tasks.
- **B:** Should-do tasks that are important but not as critical as A tasks. These tasks have mild consequences if left undone.
- **C:** Nice-to-do tasks that would be good to complete but have no significant impact on your goals. These tasks can be done after A and B tasks are completed.
- **D:** Delegate tasks that can be assigned to someone else, freeing up your time for more important work.
- **E:** Eliminate tasks that are unnecessary and don't contribute to your goals. Removing these tasks helps you focus on what truly matters.

The ABCDE Method is a quick and efficient way to prioritize your daily to-do list, ensuring that you focus on high-impact tasks first.

3. The Pareto Principle: Focus on the Vital Few

The Pareto Principle, also known as the 80/20 rule, suggests that 80% of your results come from 20% of your efforts. In other words, a small number of tasks often have a disproportionately large impact on your success. The key to using the Pareto Principle for prioritization is to identify and focus on those critical tasks that generate the most significant results.

To apply the Pareto Principle:
1. List all the tasks you need to complete.
2. Identify the top 20% of tasks that will produce 80% of your desired outcomes.
3. Prioritize these high-impact tasks, and devote most of your time and energy to completing them.

By focusing on the vital few tasks that deliver the most value, you can maximize your productivity and achieve more with less effort.

4. The Ivy Lee Method: A Daily Routine for Success

The Ivy Lee Method is a simple but powerful technique that involves creating a prioritized to-do list for each day. This method was developed by productivity consultant Ivy Lee and has been used by some of the world's most successful people.

Here's how it works:
1. At the end of each workday, write down the six most important tasks you need to accomplish the next day.
2. Prioritize these tasks in order of their importance.
3. The next day, start with the first task and work on it until it's complete. Then move on to the next task.
4. Continue working through your list until all tasks are completed or the day ends.
5. At the end of the day, move any unfinished tasks to the next day's list and repeat the process.

The Ivy Lee Method helps you stay focused on your most important tasks each day, ensuring steady progress toward your goals.

Conclusion: Mastering Prioritization

Effective prioritization is a crucial skill for anyone looking to boost their productivity and achieve their goals. By using techniques like the Eisenhower Matrix, the ABCDE Method, the Pareto Principle, and the Ivy Lee Method, you can ensure that you're always working on the tasks that matter most. These methods not only help you manage your time more effectively but also reduce stress and increase your overall sense of accomplishment. With practice, prioritization becomes second nature, allowing you to make the most of your time and achieve your ambitions with greater ease.

Balancing Short-Term and Long-Term Goals

In the pursuit of success, both short-term and long-term goals play critical roles. Short-term goals provide immediate direction and quick wins, while long-term goals represent your ultimate vision and purpose. However, balancing these two types of goals can be challenging. Focusing too much on short-term tasks may cause you to lose sight of your bigger aspirations, while being too preoccupied with long-term objectives can lead to procrastination and a lack of progress in the present. Striking the right balance between short-term and long-term goals is essential for sustained progress and fulfillment. Here's how you can achieve that balance effectively.

Understanding Short-Term Goals

Short-term goals are the tasks and objectives you aim to achieve in the near future, typically within a day, week, or few months. These goals are often more specific and immediately actionable. They provide a sense of urgency and help you build momentum toward achieving larger objectives. For example, a short-term goal might be completing a project at work, exercising three times a week, or saving a specific amount of money by the end of the month.

Short-term goals are important because they create a roadmap for your daily and weekly activities. They help you focus on immediate priorities and give you a sense of accomplishment as you check off each task. However, if you only concentrate on short-term goals, you might find yourself stuck in a cycle of busywork without making meaningful progress toward your long-term aspirations.

The Significance of Long-Term Goals

Long-term goals, on the other hand, are your broader, more significant objectives that may take years to achieve. These goals reflect your deepest desires, values, and vision for your future. Examples of long-term goals include building a successful career, achieving financial independence, mastering a new skill, or leading a healthier lifestyle.

Long-term goals provide direction and purpose, helping you stay motivated over the long haul. They serve as a guiding star, ensuring that your short-term actions are aligned with your ultimate aspirations. However, focusing too much on long-term goals can be overwhelming, leading to indecision and procrastination. Without breaking these goals into manageable steps, you might struggle to make consistent progress.

Strategies for Balancing Short-Term and Long-Term Goals

1. **Break Down Long-Term Goals into Short-Term Milestones:**
One of the most effective ways to balance short-term and long-term goals is to break down your long-term objectives into smaller, actionable milestones. For instance, if your long-term goal is to write a book, your short-term milestones might include writing a chapter each month or setting aside a specific number of hours each week for writing. By doing this, you can make steady progress toward your long-term goals while maintaining focus on immediate tasks.

2. **Prioritize with the 80/20 Rule:**
The Pareto Principle, or the 80/20 rule, suggests that 80% of your results come from 20% of your efforts. Apply this principle to your goal-setting by identifying the short-term tasks that have the most significant impact on your long-term goals. Focus on these high-impact activities to ensure that your daily efforts contribute meaningfully to your bigger vision.

3. **Use Time Blocking to Allocate Focus:**
Time blocking is a technique where you schedule specific blocks of time for different types of tasks. Dedicate certain blocks to short-term goals, such as daily tasks and immediate deadlines, and reserve other blocks for long-term planning and progress. This approach helps you balance immediate responsibilities with future aspirations, ensuring that neither is neglected.

4. **Regularly Review and Adjust Your Goals:**
Periodic review of your goals is essential for maintaining balance. Set aside time weekly or monthly to assess your progress on both short-term and long-term goals. Are your short-term efforts bringing you closer to your long-term vision? Are your long-term goals still aligned with your current values and circumstances? Regular reviews allow you to make

necessary adjustments, ensuring that your goals remain relevant and achievable.

5. **Stay Flexible and Adaptable:**
Life is unpredictable, and circumstances can change. Being too rigid with your goals can lead to frustration if things don't go as planned. Stay flexible and open to adjusting your short-term tasks and long-term objectives as needed. Adaptability is key to maintaining balance and ensuring continuous progress, even when faced with challenges.

Conclusion: Harmonizing Your Journey

Balancing short-term and long-term goals is about harmonizing your daily actions with your broader aspirations. Short-term goals provide the structure and immediate wins needed to stay motivated, while long-term goals offer the vision and purpose that guide your efforts over time. By breaking down long-term goals into manageable steps, prioritizing effectively, and regularly reviewing your progress, you can achieve a healthy balance that propels you toward success. Remember, the key to achieving your dreams lies in taking consistent, purposeful steps each day, while keeping your eyes firmly on the horizon of your ultimate goals.

Chapter 3: Time Management Strategies

The Pomodoro Technique

In today's fast-paced world, maintaining focus and productivity can be a challenge. With constant distractions from smartphones, social media, and the demands of everyday life, it's easy to lose concentration and procrastinate. The Pomodoro Technique, a time management method developed by Francesco Cirillo in the late 1980s, offers a simple yet powerful solution to this problem. This technique helps you break down your work into manageable intervals, improving focus, efficiency, and overall productivity. Here's an in-depth look at the Pomodoro Technique and how you can use it to enhance your work habits.

What is the Pomodoro Technique?

The Pomodoro Technique is named after the Italian word for "tomato," inspired by the tomato-shaped kitchen timer that Cirillo used when developing this method. At its core, the technique involves working in short, focused bursts called "Pomodoros," each followed by a brief break. The basic process is as follows:

1. **Choose a Task:** Start by selecting a task you want to work on. It could be anything from writing a report, studying for an exam, or even decluttering your workspace.

2. **Set the Timer for 25 Minutes:** Once you've chosen your task, set a timer for 25 minutes. This 25-minute work period is known as a Pomodoro. During this time, focus solely on the task at hand, avoiding any distractions.

3. **Work Until the Timer Rings:** Concentrate on your task for the entire 25 minutes. If a distraction arises, note it down and quickly return to your task. The goal is to work with full concentration until the timer rings.

4. **Take a Short Break:** After the 25-minute Pomodoro session, take a 5-minute break. Use this time to relax, stretch, grab a snack, or simply take a mental break from your work.

5. **Repeat the Process:** After completing four Pomodoros (a total of 100 minutes of focused work), take a longer break of 15-30 minutes. This extended break allows you to recharge before starting the next round of Pomodoros.

Why the Pomodoro Technique Works

The Pomodoro Technique is effective for several reasons. First, it leverages the power of timeboxing, where tasks are confined to a specific timeframe, reducing the temptation to procrastinate. Knowing you only have 25 minutes to work before a break makes it easier to stay focused and dive into the task.

Second, the technique encourages frequent breaks, which are essential for maintaining mental energy and preventing burnout. Regular breaks help refresh your mind, making it easier to sustain high levels of concentration throughout the day.

Third, the Pomodoro Technique helps you overcome perfectionism by promoting a "just start" mentality. Since you only have to commit to 25 minutes at a time, it's easier to begin tasks that might otherwise seem daunting. Once you start, momentum often carries you forward, making it easier to continue working beyond the first Pomodoro.

Benefits of the Pomodoro Technique

1. **Enhanced Focus:** By dedicating 25 minutes to a single task, the Pomodoro Technique minimizes distractions and helps you enter a state of deep focus, also known as flow. This leads to higher quality work and greater efficiency.

2. **Better Time Management:** The technique helps you structure your day into manageable chunks, making it easier to allocate time to various tasks and prioritize effectively. It also allows you to track how much time you spend on different activities, giving you insights into your work habits.

3. **Reduced Procrastination:** The Pomodoro Technique makes it easier to start tasks, even those you've been putting off. The short, timed intervals create a sense of urgency, helping you overcome the inertia of procrastination.

4. **Improved Work-Life Balance:** Regular breaks prevent burnout and help you maintain a healthy work-life balance. By using the technique, you can work more efficiently, leaving more time for leisure and relaxation.

5. **Increased Productivity:** The combination of focused work sessions and regular breaks leads to higher productivity. You're able to accomplish more in less time, without sacrificing the quality of your work.

How to Implement the Pomodoro Technique

To get started with the Pomodoro Technique, all you need is a timer and a task list. Many people use physical timers, but there are also numerous apps and digital timers specifically designed for this technique. Start with the classic 25/5-minute structure, but feel free to adjust the intervals to suit your needs. Some people find that longer work sessions, such as 50 minutes followed by a 10-minute break, work better for them.

As you become more comfortable with the technique, you can experiment with different tasks and work environments to maximize your productivity. The key is to remain consistent and committed to the process, allowing the technique to become a natural part of your daily routine.

Conclusion: A Simple Yet Powerful Tool

The Pomodoro Technique is a simple yet powerful tool that can transform the way you work. By breaking your day into focused intervals, you can improve your concentration, manage your time more effectively, and reduce the stress associated with overwhelming tasks. Whether you're a student, a professional, or anyone looking to enhance their productivity, the Pomodoro Technique offers a practical and adaptable approach to getting things done. Give it a try, and you may find that those 25-minute intervals become some of the most productive moments of your day.

Time Blocking and Scheduling

Time is one of the most valuable resources we have, yet it's often squandered through distractions, poor planning, and lack of focus. If you've ever felt overwhelmed by your to-do list or frustrated by how quickly the day slips away without accomplishing much, you're not alone. One powerful method to regain control over your time and boost productivity is through time blocking and scheduling. These techniques help you structure your day, prioritize tasks, and ensure that your most important activities get the attention they deserve. Here's how time blocking and scheduling can revolutionize the way you work.

What is Time Blocking?

Time blocking is a time management method where you divide your day into discrete blocks of time, each dedicated to a specific task or group of tasks. Instead of working from an open-ended to-do list, you schedule when you'll work on each task throughout your day. This approach not only helps you focus on one task at a time but also ensures that all your important activities are accounted for in your daily schedule.

For example, instead of writing "work on report" on your to-do list, you would block off a specific time in your calendar, say from 9:00 AM to 10:30 AM, exclusively for working on that report. Once that block of time starts, you focus solely on the task at hand, avoiding distractions and multitasking.

The Benefits of Time Blocking

1. **Improved Focus and Productivity:**
   Time blocking helps eliminate distractions by assigning specific times for each task. When you know that a certain block of time is reserved for a particular activity, you're less likely to check your phone, browse the internet, or get sidetracked by other tasks. This focused approach increases your efficiency and allows you to accomplish more in less time.

2. **Better Time Management:**
   By planning your day in advance and allocating time for each task, you gain a clear picture of how your time is spent. This helps you make

better decisions about how to prioritize your activities, ensuring that your most important tasks are completed first. It also prevents tasks from dragging on indefinitely, as you have a set timeframe to complete them.

3. **Reduced Overwhelm and Stress:**
Time blocking provides structure to your day, which can reduce feelings of overwhelm. Instead of juggling multiple tasks at once, you can focus on one thing at a time, knowing that everything else has its own designated slot. This organization reduces the mental load and helps you stay calm and collected throughout the day.

4. **Increased Accountability:**
When you commit to time blocking, you hold yourself accountable to your schedule. It becomes easier to stick to your plans and resist the temptation to procrastinate. Over time, this discipline leads to a more consistent and productive work routine.

How to Implement Time Blocking

1. **Start with Your Priorities:**
Begin by identifying your most important tasks for the day or week. These could be work-related projects, personal commitments, or anything that requires your focus. Once you've listed your priorities, estimate how much time each task will take.

2. **Create a Schedule:**
Open your calendar and begin blocking off time for each task. Start with your highest priorities, placing them during your peak productivity hours. For example, if you're most focused in the morning, schedule your most challenging tasks then. Be realistic about how much time each task will take, and leave some buffer time between blocks to account for unexpected delays.

3. **Include Breaks and Downtime:**
It's crucial to schedule breaks and downtime into your day. This not only helps you recharge but also prevents burnout. For example, after a 90-minute work block, you might schedule a 10-minute break to stretch,

grab a snack, or simply relax. Regular breaks can actually boost your productivity by keeping your mind fresh and focused.

4. **Stick to Your Schedule:**
Once you've created your schedule, the key is to stick to it as closely as possible. Treat each time block as an appointment you can't miss. If distractions arise, make a note of them and address them during a scheduled break or at the end of the day. The more you practice sticking to your schedule, the more natural it will become.

5. **Review and Adjust:**
At the end of each day or week, review how well your time blocking worked. Did you accomplish what you set out to do? Were there tasks that took longer than expected? Use this reflection to adjust your future time blocks. Over time, you'll become more accurate in estimating how long tasks take and better at creating a schedule that works for you.

Conclusion: Take Control of Your Time

Time blocking and scheduling are powerful tools for taking control of your day and making the most of your time. By deliberately planning how you'll spend each hour, you can prioritize your most important tasks, stay focused, and reduce the stress that comes with trying to juggle too many things at once. This method not only helps you get more done but also improves the quality of your work and your overall well-being. If you're looking to boost your productivity and bring more structure to your day, give time blocking a try. With a bit of practice, you'll find that it's one of the most effective ways to manage your time and achieve your goals.

Overcoming Procrastination

Procrastination is a challenge that almost everyone faces at some point. It's that frustrating habit of putting off important tasks until the last minute, only to be overwhelmed by stress as deadlines approach. Procrastination can take many forms—delaying work, avoiding decisions, or endlessly postponing personal goals. Despite knowing the negative impact of procrastination, many people find it difficult to overcome. However, with the right strategies and mindset, it is possible to break free from the cycle of procrastination and regain control over your time and productivity. Here's how you can do it.

Understanding the Roots of Procrastination

Before diving into strategies to overcome procrastination, it's important to understand why it happens in the first place. Procrastination often stems from a combination of psychological factors:

1. **Fear of Failure:** Many people procrastinate because they fear not being able to complete a task successfully. This fear can cause them to avoid starting the task altogether, leading to last-minute panic and subpar results.

2. **Perfectionism:** The desire to do something perfectly can also lead to procrastination. When you set unrealistically high standards, you might delay starting a task because you're afraid it won't meet those standards.

3. **Lack of Motivation:** When a task seems uninteresting or lacks immediate rewards, it can be hard to find the motivation to start. This lack of motivation often leads to postponing the task in favor of more enjoyable activities.

4. **Overwhelm:** Sometimes, tasks seem so large or complex that they feel overwhelming. When faced with such tasks, people often procrastinate because they don't know where to begin.

5. **Distractions:** In today's world, distractions are everywhere—social media, emails, and constant notifications can easily pull you away from your work. These distractions make it easy to procrastinate, even when you have the best intentions to focus.

Strategies to Overcome Procrastination

1. **Break Tasks into Smaller Steps:**
   One of the most effective ways to overcome procrastination is to break large tasks into smaller, more manageable steps. When a task feels overwhelming, breaking it down can make it feel more approachable. For example, if you need to write a report, start by outlining the main sections, then focus on writing one section at a time. Each small step will bring you closer to completing the task, making it easier to start and maintain momentum.

2. **Use the Two-Minute Rule:**
   The Two-Minute Rule, popularized by productivity expert David Allen, suggests that if a task takes less than two minutes to complete, do it immediately. This rule helps eliminate small tasks that can accumulate and become overwhelming. By taking care of these quick tasks right away, you can prevent them from becoming a source of procrastination.

3. **Set Realistic Goals:**
   Perfectionism often leads to procrastination, so it's important to set realistic, achievable goals. Instead of aiming for perfection, focus on making progress. Set specific, measurable goals that are challenging yet attainable. This approach reduces the pressure to be perfect and encourages you to take action.

4. **Create a Reward System:**
   Motivation plays a crucial role in overcoming procrastination. One way to boost motivation is to create a reward system for yourself. For example, after completing a difficult task, treat yourself to something you enjoy, like a favorite snack, a short walk, or time spent on a hobby. Rewards provide positive reinforcement, making it easier to start and complete tasks in the future.

5. **Eliminate Distractions:**
   Distractions are a major cause of procrastination, so it's important to create a work environment that minimizes them. Turn off unnecessary notifications, close unrelated tabs on your computer, and find a quiet space where you can focus. If you struggle with staying off social media, consider using apps or browser extensions that block access during work hours.

6. **Practice Time Management Techniques:**
   Effective time management can help you overcome procrastination by structuring your day and prioritizing tasks. Techniques like time blocking, where you schedule specific times for each task, can be particularly helpful. By allocating time for each activity, you create a sense of urgency and make it easier to start tasks without delay.

7. **Forgive Yourself for Past Procrastination:**
   Beating yourself up over past procrastination can create a negative cycle of guilt and more procrastination. Instead, acknowledge your past behavior, forgive yourself, and focus on what you can do differently moving forward. Self-compassion is key to breaking the cycle and building better habits.

The Power of Taking Action

The most important step in overcoming procrastination is simply to start. Taking even the smallest action can create momentum, making it easier to continue working on a task. Remember, progress is more important than perfection, and each step you take brings you closer to your goals. By understanding the underlying causes of procrastination and applying these strategies, you can break free from the habit and become more productive, focused, and successful.

Procrastination may be a common challenge, but it doesn't have to define your work habits or your life. With patience, practice, and persistence, you can overcome procrastination and unlock your full potential.

Chapter 4: Tools and Techniques

Productivity Apps and Software

In today's digital age, staying productive can be a challenge with the constant barrage of notifications, emails, and online distractions. However, technology also offers solutions in the form of productivity apps and software that can help you manage your time, organize tasks, and stay focused on what truly matters. Whether you're a student, a professional, or someone simply looking to get more out of your day, these tools can significantly enhance your efficiency and productivity. Here's a closer look at how productivity apps and software can transform the way you work.

The Role of Productivity Apps

Productivity apps and software are designed to help you streamline your tasks, reduce inefficiencies, and make the most of your time. They come in various forms, each targeting different aspects of productivity:

1. **Task Management:** These apps help you create, organize, and prioritize your tasks. Examples include **Todoist**, **Trello**, and **Microsoft To Do**. With these tools, you can break down your projects into smaller tasks, set deadlines, and track your progress. The visual nature of task management apps makes it easier to see what needs to be done and when, helping you stay on top of your workload.

2. **Time Management:** Apps like **Toggl** and **RescueTime** help you monitor how you spend your time. By tracking the amount of time you dedicate to different tasks, these apps provide insights into your work habits, allowing you to identify time-wasting activities and areas where you can improve. Time management apps are especially useful for those who want to optimize their productivity by ensuring that their time is spent on high-priority tasks.

3. **Focus and Distraction Management:** Tools like **Forest** and **Focus@Will** are designed to minimize distractions and help you maintain concentration. **Forest**, for example, encourages you to stay off your phone by growing a virtual tree that will die if you leave the app.

Focus@Will uses specially designed music tracks to enhance focus and productivity, making it easier to stay in the zone while working.

4. **Note-Taking and Organization:** Apps like **Evernote**, **Notion**, and **Microsoft OneNote** allow you to capture ideas, organize notes, and store important information in a centralized location. These apps often include features like tagging, searching, and cross-device syncing, making it easy to access your notes wherever you are. They're particularly useful for students, researchers, and professionals who need to keep track of large amounts of information.

5. **Collaboration Tools:** For teams, productivity software like **Slack**, **Asana**, and **Monday.com** enable seamless communication and collaboration. These tools allow team members to share files, assign tasks, and discuss projects in real-time, reducing the need for endless email threads and meetings. By keeping everyone on the same page, collaboration tools help teams work more efficiently and effectively.

How to Choose the Right Productivity App

With so many productivity apps and software available, choosing the right one can be overwhelming. Here are a few tips to help you make the best choice:

1. **Identify Your Needs:** Start by determining what you need help with. Are you struggling with time management, task organization, or staying focused? Understanding your specific needs will help you narrow down the options and choose an app that addresses your biggest challenges.

2. **Consider Ease of Use:** The best productivity app is one that you'll actually use. Look for apps with intuitive interfaces and features that align with your workflow. Avoid apps that are overly complex or require a steep learning curve, as this may discourage you from using them consistently.

3. **Check Compatibility:** Ensure that the app you choose is compatible with your devices and integrates well with the other tools you

use. For example, if you use Google Calendar for scheduling, you might want to choose a task management app that syncs with it seamlessly.

4. **Trial and Error:** Don't be afraid to try out a few different apps before settling on one. Many productivity apps offer free trials or basic versions, allowing you to test their features and see if they meet your needs before committing to a paid plan.

5. **Read Reviews and Recommendations:** User reviews and expert recommendations can provide valuable insights into the strengths and weaknesses of different apps. Look for feedback on the app's reliability, customer support, and overall effectiveness in improving productivity.

The Benefits of Using Productivity Apps

1. **Enhanced Organization:** Productivity apps help you keep track of your tasks, deadlines, and notes in an organized manner. This reduces the likelihood of forgetting important tasks and makes it easier to prioritize your work.

2. **Better Time Management:** By tracking your time and eliminating distractions, productivity apps help you manage your time more effectively. You'll be able to see where your time is going and make adjustments to ensure you're focusing on the most important tasks.

3. **Increased Focus:** Distraction-blocking features and focus-enhancing tools help you maintain concentration, making it easier to complete tasks without getting sidetracked.

4. **Improved Collaboration:** For teams, productivity software streamlines communication and project management, ensuring that everyone is on the same page and working towards the same goals.

5. **Reduced Stress:** When you have a clear plan for your day and the tools to stay organized, you're less likely to feel overwhelmed by your workload. Productivity apps help you approach your tasks with confidence, reducing stress and improving your overall well-being.

Conclusion: Embrace the Power of Productivity Apps

Productivity apps and software are invaluable tools that can help you take control of your time, stay organized, and work more efficiently. By choosing the right apps for your needs and incorporating them into your daily routine, you can overcome procrastination, manage your tasks more effectively, and ultimately achieve your goals with greater ease. In a world full of distractions, these digital tools offer a path to enhanced focus, better time management, and a more productive life. Whether you're working on a big project, managing a team, or simply trying to get through your to-do list, productivity apps can make a significant difference in how you approach your work and your life.

Task Management Systems

In a world where juggling multiple responsibilities is the norm, staying organized and on top of your workload is crucial. Task management systems are tools designed to help you efficiently manage your tasks, projects, and goals, ensuring that nothing falls through the cracks. Whether you're a busy professional, a student with numerous assignments, or someone trying to balance work and personal life, a task management system can be your key to staying productive and reducing stress. Here's a comprehensive guide to understanding task management systems and how they can revolutionize the way you work.

What Are Task Management Systems?

A task management system is a software tool or platform that helps individuals and teams plan, track, and complete tasks. These systems allow you to break down larger projects into manageable tasks, set deadlines, prioritize work, and monitor progress. At their core, task management systems provide a structured way to organize your workload, making it easier to focus on what needs to be done and when.

Key Features of Task Management Systems

1. **Task Creation and Organization:**
   Task management systems allow you to create individual tasks and organize them into projects or categories. This helps you see all the work you need to do in one place. You can add details like descriptions, due dates, attachments, and subtasks, making it easier to manage complex projects.

2. **Prioritization and Deadlines:**
   One of the main benefits of task management systems is the ability to prioritize tasks and set deadlines. By assigning priority levels to tasks (e.g., high, medium, low), you can ensure that the most important tasks are tackled first. Deadlines help you stay on track and avoid last-minute rushes.

3. **Progress Tracking:**
   These systems often include features that allow you to track your progress. For example, you can mark tasks as "in progress" or "completed" and see how much of a project is done. Some systems even offer visual progress indicators, like percentage bars or Kanban boards, which provide a clear overview of where you stand with your tasks.

4. **Collaboration Tools:**
   For teams, task management systems offer collaboration features that enable multiple users to work together on projects. Team members can assign tasks to each other, share updates, and leave comments. This fosters better communication and ensures that everyone is on the same page.

5. **Notifications and Reminders:**
   To help you stay on top of deadlines, task management systems often include notification and reminder features. You can receive alerts when a deadline is approaching, or when a task has been assigned to you, ensuring that important tasks aren't overlooked.

6. **Integration with Other Tools:**
   Many task management systems integrate with other productivity tools like calendars, email, and file storage services. This allows for seamless

workflow management and ensures that all your tools work together in harmony.

Popular Task Management Systems

There are numerous task management systems available, each with its unique features and strengths. Here are some popular options:

1. **Trello:**
   Trello uses a visual system of boards, lists, and cards to organize tasks. It's highly intuitive and is great for individuals and small teams who prefer a visual approach to task management. You can easily drag and drop cards to different lists, making it simple to track progress.

2. **Asana:**
   Asana is a robust task management tool that is ideal for teams. It allows users to create projects, assign tasks, set due dates, and track progress. Asana's powerful collaboration features and integrations make it a popular choice for larger projects.

3. **Todoist:**
   Todoist is a simple yet powerful task management app that helps you organize your tasks and projects across devices. It offers features like due dates, priorities, labels, and productivity tracking, making it a great tool for both personal and professional use.

4. **Microsoft To Do:**
   Microsoft To Do integrates seamlessly with other Microsoft products like Outlook and Teams, making it a convenient choice for those already using Microsoft's suite of tools. It's user-friendly and offers basic task management features like lists, reminders, and due dates.

5. **Notion:**
   Notion is an all-in-one workspace that combines task management with note-taking, databases, and collaboration tools. It's highly customizable, allowing users to create personalized workflows that suit their needs.

Benefits of Using a Task Management System

1. **Increased Productivity:**
   Task management systems help you stay organized, prioritize your work, and manage your time effectively. By having a clear overview of your tasks and deadlines, you can focus on what matters most and avoid wasting time on less important activities.

2. **Reduced Stress:**
   When all your tasks are organized in a system, you don't have to worry about forgetting something important. This peace of mind reduces stress and allows you to approach your work with a clearer, more focused mindset.

3. **Better Collaboration:**
   For teams, task management systems enhance collaboration by providing a central place where everyone can see what needs to be done and who is responsible for each task. This transparency reduces misunderstandings and ensures that projects move forward smoothly.

4. **Improved Accountability:**
   By assigning tasks and setting deadlines, task management systems create a sense of accountability. Everyone knows what they need to do and when, making it easier to track progress and hold yourself and others accountable for completing tasks on time.

How to Choose the Right Task Management System

1. **Assess Your Needs:**
   Consider what you need from a task management system. Are you managing personal tasks, or do you need a tool for team collaboration? Do you prefer a visual interface, or do you need advanced features like time tracking and integrations?

2. **Test Multiple Options:**
   Many task management systems offer free trials or basic versions. Test a few different tools to see which one fits your workflow best. Pay

attention to ease of use, interface design, and whether the tool feels intuitive to you.

3. **Consider Your Budget:**
   While some task management systems are free, others offer premium features at a cost. Consider your budget and decide if the additional features are worth the investment.

Conclusion: Master Your Tasks with the Right System

Task management systems are essential tools for anyone looking to stay organized, productive, and stress-free. By choosing the right system and incorporating it into your daily routine, you can manage your workload more effectively, meet deadlines, and achieve your goals with greater ease. Whether you're working alone or as part of a team, a task management system can help you stay on track and get more done, making it a valuable addition to your productivity toolkit.

The Power of Checklists

In our fast-paced world, where juggling multiple tasks and responsibilities is the norm, it's easy to feel overwhelmed. From work assignments and household chores to personal goals, the sheer volume of things we need to keep track of can be daunting. This is where the humble checklist comes into play—a simple yet incredibly powerful tool that can transform how you manage your time and tasks. Although checklists might seem basic, their impact on productivity, organization, and even mental clarity is profound. Let's explore why checklists are so effective and how you can harness their power to streamline your life.

Why Checklists Work

Checklists work because they break down complex tasks into manageable steps, providing a clear roadmap for getting things done. The simplicity of a checklist is its greatest strength. Here's why:

1. **Clarity and Focus**:
   When you create a checklist, you're essentially mapping out a plan of action. Each item on the list represents a specific step you need to take, which helps eliminate confusion about what to do next. This clarity allows you to focus on one task at a time, reducing the chances of becoming overwhelmed by the bigger picture.

2. **Reduced Cognitive Load**:
   Our brains are not designed to hold and process large amounts of information simultaneously. Trying to remember every task you need to complete can lead to mental fatigue and stress. A checklist serves as an external memory aid, freeing up mental space and reducing the cognitive load on your brain. This not only makes you more efficient but also reduces the likelihood of forgetting important tasks.

3. **Increased Productivity**:
   Checklists provide a visual representation of progress. As you check off each item, you get a sense of accomplishment, which can be incredibly motivating. This positive reinforcement encourages you to keep going, increasing your overall productivity. The satisfaction of ticking off completed tasks creates a momentum that helps you power through your to-do list.

4. **Improved Accuracy and Consistency**:
   In professions where precision is crucial, such as medicine, aviation, or engineering, checklists are used to ensure that no critical steps are missed. By following a checklist, you can maintain a high level of accuracy and consistency in your work, whether you're performing a routine task or tackling a complex project. This reduces the risk of errors and ensures that all necessary steps are completed.

5. **Stress Reduction**:
   Knowing exactly what you need to do and having a plan to get it done can significantly reduce stress. A checklist helps you stay organized and in control, preventing the anxiety that often comes with having too much to do and not enough time. When you can see that progress is being made, even if it's one small step at a time, it can provide peace of mind.

How to Create Effective Checklists

While creating a checklist may seem straightforward, there are some best practices to follow to ensure that your checklists are as effective as possible:

1. **Be Specific**:
   Break down tasks into specific, actionable items. For example, instead of writing "work on project," break it down into smaller tasks like "outline project plan," "research topic," and "draft first section." Specific tasks are easier to start and complete, making your checklist more manageable.

2. **Prioritize Tasks**:
   Not all tasks are created equal. Prioritize your checklist by identifying which tasks are most important or time-sensitive. You can use numbering, color-coding, or symbols to indicate priority levels. This helps you focus on what needs to be done first and ensures that critical tasks don't get overlooked.

3. **Keep It Realistic**:
   A checklist should be a tool for productivity, not a source of stress. Avoid overloading your checklist with too many tasks. Be realistic about what you can accomplish in a day or a specific period. If your checklist is too long, it can become overwhelming, which defeats its purpose.

4. **Review and Update Regularly**:
   Checklists are not set in stone. Review and update your checklist regularly to reflect any changes in your priorities or new tasks that arise. This keeps your checklist relevant and ensures that you're always working on the most important tasks.

5. **Use the Right Tools**:
   While a simple piece of paper can work for a checklist, there are many digital tools available that offer additional features like reminders, due dates, and the ability to sync across devices. Apps like Todoist, Microsoft To Do, or even the notes app on your phone can help you create and manage your checklists more efficiently.

The Versatility of Checklists

Checklists are incredibly versatile and can be used in virtually every aspect of life. Here are a few examples:

1. **Daily Task Lists**:
    A daily checklist helps you stay on top of your daily responsibilities. From work-related tasks to personal errands, a daily checklist ensures that you don't forget anything important.

2. **Project Management**:
    For larger projects, a checklist can help you break down the project into manageable phases. You can create separate checklists for each phase, ensuring that every aspect of the project is covered.

3. **Packing for Trips**:
    A travel checklist ensures that you don't forget any essentials when packing for a trip. From clothing to toiletries and travel documents, a checklist can make the packing process stress-free.

4. **Event Planning**:
    Whether you're planning a wedding, a party, or a business event, a checklist helps you keep track of all the details—from booking a venue to sending out invitations.

5. **Learning and Development**:
    Use checklists to track your progress on learning new skills or achieving personal goals. Breaking down your goals into actionable steps can make them more attainable.

Conclusion: The Simple Power of Checklists

The power of checklists lies in their simplicity and effectiveness. By providing structure, clarity, and a sense of accomplishment, checklists can transform how you approach tasks and projects. Whether you're managing daily responsibilities or working on complex projects, checklists can help you stay organized, reduce stress, and improve productivity. Embracing the habit of using checklists can lead to more efficient work habits, better outcomes, and a greater sense of control over your life. So, the next time you feel overwhelmed by your to-do list, remember that the solution might be as simple as breaking it down into a checklist.

Chapter 5: Habits and Routines

Building Productive Habits

Building productive habits is one of the most powerful ways to achieve long-term success and well-being. While motivation can get you started, it's habits that will carry you through the challenges and obstacles that inevitably arise. Habits are the small, consistent actions you take every day that, over time, accumulate into significant results. But forming these habits doesn't happen overnight. It requires intentionality, patience, and the right strategies. Here's a deep dive into how you can build productive habits that stick, leading to a more fulfilling and accomplished life.

Why Habits Matter

Habits are powerful because they automate behaviors, reducing the mental energy required to make decisions. Once a habit is established, it becomes a part of your routine, allowing you to perform it with little thought. This frees up your mental resources for more complex tasks and decisions. Productive habits can help you achieve goals, improve your health, enhance your skills, and boost your overall quality of life. Whether it's exercising regularly, reading daily, or managing your time effectively, the right habits can lead to significant positive changes.

The Science of Habit Formation

Habits are formed through a process known as the habit loop, which consists of three main components: the cue, the routine, and the reward.

1. **Cue:** The cue is the trigger that initiates the habit. It can be a time of day, an emotional state, or a specific situation. For example, waking up in the morning might be the cue for your habit of brushing your teeth.

2. **Routine:** The routine is the behavior or action that you perform in response to the cue. This is the habit itself—such as going for a jog, writing in your journal, or starting your workday with a planning session.

3. **Reward:** The reward is the positive reinforcement you receive after completing the routine. It can be a feeling of accomplishment, the satisfaction of ticking off a task, or even a small treat you give yourself.

Understanding this loop is key to building new habits. By consciously linking a cue to a routine and ensuring there's a reward, you can start to establish a habit that will eventually become automatic.

Strategies for Building Productive Habits

1. **Start Small:**
   One of the biggest mistakes people make when trying to build a new habit is starting too big. If your goal is to read more, don't aim to read an entire book in a week right away. Start with just 10 pages a day. By starting small, you make the habit easy to stick to, which builds momentum over time.

2. **Be Consistent:**
   Consistency is the key to habit formation. It's better to do something small every day than to do something big sporadically. For example, if you want to develop the habit of writing, it's more effective to write for 10 minutes every day than to try and write for two hours once a week. Consistent action helps solidify the habit loop in your brain.

3. **Use Triggers:**
A trigger or cue can help you remember to perform your habit. This could be something you already do regularly, like drinking your morning coffee or brushing your teeth. Attach the new habit to an existing one. For example, if you want to start meditating, do it right after you brush your teeth in the morning. This way, brushing your teeth becomes the cue for meditation.

4. **Track Your Progress:**
Keeping track of your habit can provide motivation and accountability. You can use a habit tracker app, a journal, or even just a calendar where you mark off each day you complete the habit. Seeing your progress visually can be incredibly motivating and helps reinforce the habit loop.

5. **Reward Yourself:**
The reward is a crucial part of the habit loop. It doesn't have to be anything extravagant—a simple acknowledgment of your accomplishment can be enough. For example, after completing your workout, take a few minutes to relax and enjoy a healthy snack. The reward reinforces the habit and makes it more likely you'll stick with it.

6. **Be Patient and Persistent:**
Building habits takes time. Studies suggest it can take anywhere from 21 to 66 days to establish a new habit, depending on its complexity. Don't get discouraged if you don't see immediate results. Persistence is key. If you miss a day, don't let it derail your progress—simply get back on track the next day.

7. **Surround Yourself with Positive Influences:**
Your environment plays a significant role in habit formation. Surround yourself with people who support your goals or who have similar habits. Positive influences can encourage you to stay on track and provide inspiration when you need it most.

Overcoming Common Challenges

Even with the best intentions, building new habits can be challenging. Here are a few common obstacles and how to overcome them:

1. **Lack of Motivation:**
   If you find your motivation waning, remind yourself of why you started. Visualize the benefits of sticking to the habit and how it will improve your life. Sometimes, motivation comes after you start—so begin the task, even if you don't feel like it.

2. **Time Constraints:**
   If you're struggling to find time for your new habit, reevaluate your schedule. Look for small pockets of time that you can dedicate to your habit. Remember, even five minutes a day is better than nothing.

3. **Perfectionism:**
   Don't let the desire for perfection prevent you from making progress. Accept that you won't be perfect and that it's okay to have off days. Focus on consistency and improvement over time, rather than immediate perfection.

Conclusion: The Long-Term Impact of Productive Habits

Building productive habits is one of the most effective ways to create lasting change in your life. By understanding the habit loop, starting small, and being consistent, you can gradually build habits that lead to significant improvements in your productivity, health, and overall well-being. Remember that habit formation is a journey—one that requires patience, persistence, and self-compassion. The effort you put into building these habits today will pay off in the long run, helping you achieve your goals and live a more fulfilling life.

Morning and Evening Routines

Establishing effective morning and evening routines can be a game-changer in enhancing productivity, mental clarity, and overall well-being. These routines set the tone for your day and help you wind down in the evening, creating a balanced rhythm that promotes success in both personal and professional areas of life. When done correctly, morning and evening routines can serve as powerful tools to align your actions with your goals, reduce stress, and ensure that you make the most of your time.

The Power of a Morning Routine

Your morning routine is crucial because it sets the tone for the rest of your day. Starting your day with intention helps you feel more in control and prepares you to tackle whatever comes your way. Here's how you can craft a morning routine that primes you for success:

1. **Wake Up Early:**
   Waking up early gives you a head start on your day. It provides quiet time to focus on yourself before the demands of the day begin. An early start also allows you to accomplish more before most people even get out of bed, creating a sense of accomplishment that can boost your confidence and energy levels throughout the day.

2. **Practice Mindfulness:**
   Begin your day with mindfulness practices such as meditation, deep breathing, or journaling. This helps clear your mind, reduce stress, and set a positive, calm tone for the day ahead. Even just five minutes of mindfulness can make a significant difference in how you handle the day's challenges.

3. **Exercise:**
   Incorporating physical activity into your morning routine is a great way to energize your body and mind. Exercise releases endorphins, which can improve your mood and mental clarity. Whether it's a full workout, a brisk walk, or some light stretching, moving your body in the morning can set a positive momentum for the rest of the day.

4. **Eat a Healthy Breakfast:**
   A nutritious breakfast fuels your body and mind, providing the energy you need to stay focused and productive. Opt for balanced meals that include protein, whole grains, and fruits or vegetables. This ensures that your body has the nutrients it needs to perform optimally.

5. **Plan Your Day:**
   Take a few minutes to review your goals and tasks for the day. Prioritize your tasks and create a to-do list that outlines what you need to accomplish. This helps you stay organized and focused, making it easier to manage your time effectively. When you start the day with a clear plan, you're less likely to get sidetracked by distractions.

The Importance of an Evening Routine

Just as a morning routine sets the stage for a successful day, an evening routine helps you wind down, reflect, and prepare for tomorrow. It's a time to transition from the busyness of the day to a state of relaxation and rest. Here's how you can create an evening routine that supports rest and rejuvenation:

1. **Unplug from Technology:**
   Reduce your screen time at least an hour before bed. The blue light emitted by screens can interfere with your body's production of melatonin, the hormone that regulates sleep. Instead of scrolling through your phone or watching TV, opt for activities that promote relaxation, such as reading a book, listening to calming music, or practicing mindfulness.

2. **Reflect on Your Day:**
   Spend a few minutes reflecting on your day. Consider what went well, what you could improve, and what you're grateful for. This practice of reflection can help you learn from your experiences and approach the next day with a positive mindset. Journaling is a great way to capture these reflections and track your personal growth over time.

3. **Prepare for Tomorrow:**
   Reduce morning stress by preparing for the next day in advance. Lay out your clothes, pack your bag, and review your schedule. This not only saves time in the morning but also gives you peace of mind, knowing that you're organized and ready for the day ahead.

4. **Practice Relaxation Techniques:**

Engage in activities that help you unwind and signal to your body that it's time to sleep. This could include taking a warm bath, practicing gentle yoga, or doing deep breathing exercises. Relaxation techniques help lower your stress levels and prepare your body and mind for restful sleep.

5. **Set a Consistent Bedtime:**
Going to bed at the same time each night helps regulate your body's internal clock, making it easier to fall asleep and wake up naturally. Aim for 7-9 hours of sleep per night to ensure you're fully rested and ready to take on the day. Consistency in your sleep schedule is key to maintaining your energy levels and overall health.

Integrating Morning and Evening Routines

To maximize the benefits of your routines, it's important to see them as a continuous cycle rather than two separate entities. Your evening routine sets the foundation for a successful morning, and your morning routine helps you navigate the day effectively, leading to a productive evening.

For example, if you plan your day and prepare for tomorrow during your evening routine, you'll wake up feeling more organized and less rushed. Similarly, starting your morning with mindfulness and exercise can help you approach your evening with a sense of accomplishment, making it easier to relax and unwind.

Conclusion: The Lasting Impact of Routines

Morning and evening routines are more than just daily rituals—they're powerful tools for personal development and productivity. By establishing routines that align with your goals and values, you create a framework that supports success, reduces stress, and enhances your overall well-being. The key is to be consistent, patient, and flexible. As you refine your routines, you'll find that these small, daily actions can lead to significant, lasting changes in your life. Whether you're aiming for better health, improved focus, or greater peace of mind, a well-structured morning and evening routine can help you achieve those goals and more.

The Role of Discipline and Consistency

Discipline and consistency are two of the most crucial elements for achieving success in any area of life. While talent and luck can play a part, it's the steadfast application of discipline and the relentless pursuit of consistency that often separate those who merely aspire from those who actually achieve. Understanding and mastering these principles can lead to remarkable results, whether in your personal life, career, or relationships. Let's delve into why discipline and consistency are so vital and how they can be effectively cultivated.

Discipline: The Foundation of Success

Discipline is the ability to do what needs to be done, even when you don't feel like doing it. It's about making choices that align with your long-term goals rather than succumbing to immediate desires or distractions. Discipline is often seen as a form of self-control, but it's more than that—it's a commitment to your future self. Here's why discipline is indispensable:

1. **Focus on Long-Term Goals:**
   Discipline helps you stay focused on your long-term objectives, even when the journey is tough. Whether you're trying to build a new habit, complete a project, or improve your health, discipline keeps you on track. It prevents you from being swayed by short-term temptations or distractions, ensuring that your actions are aligned with your ultimate goals.

2. **Overcoming Procrastination:**
   One of the biggest obstacles to productivity is procrastination. Discipline allows you to push past the urge to delay tasks. It helps you take action, even when motivation is low or when the task seems daunting. By consistently practicing discipline, you train your mind to

prioritize action over inaction, which can significantly increase your efficiency and productivity.

3. **Building Character and Resilience:**
   Discipline is closely linked to resilience—the ability to keep going despite setbacks. When you practice discipline regularly, you build mental toughness and develop the capacity to endure challenges without giving up. This resilience is crucial for navigating the inevitable ups and downs of life.

4. **Maintaining Integrity:**
   Discipline ensures that you stay true to your values and commitments, even when it's difficult. It helps you uphold your promises to yourself and others, fostering a sense of integrity and trustworthiness. This integrity is not only important for personal growth but also for building strong, reliable relationships.

Consistency: The Key to Sustained Progress

While discipline gets you started, consistency is what keeps you going. Consistency is about showing up, day in and day out, regardless of circumstances. It's the steady application of effort over time that leads to significant, lasting results. Here's why consistency is so important:

1. **Compounding Effect:**
   Consistency is like the compound interest of self-improvement. Small actions, repeated consistently over time, accumulate and lead to significant results. Whether it's exercising regularly, studying daily, or working towards a goal bit by bit, consistency allows your efforts to build on each other, leading to exponential growth.

2. **Building Habits:**
   Consistency is the cornerstone of habit formation. It's through repetition that actions become automatic. By consistently practicing a behavior, you embed it into your daily routine, making it easier to maintain in the long run. This is crucial for developing positive habits that support your goals.

3. **Creating Momentum:**
   When you're consistent, you create momentum. Each small victory or completed task adds to your forward motion, making it easier to continue. This momentum can help you overcome challenges and push through periods of low motivation. Once you establish a rhythm, consistency becomes its own source of motivation.

4. **Establishing Trust:**
   Consistency also plays a critical role in relationships, whether personal or professional. When you consistently show up and deliver on your promises, you build trust and credibility. People learn that they can rely on you, which strengthens your relationships and opens up new opportunities.

How to Cultivate Discipline and Consistency

1. **Set Clear Goals:**
   The first step to cultivating discipline and consistency is to set clear, achievable goals. When you have a clear direction, it's easier to stay disciplined and consistent because you know what you're working towards. Break your goals down into smaller, manageable steps to make the process less overwhelming.

2. **Create a Routine:**
   Establishing a daily routine can help you maintain discipline and consistency. When certain tasks become part of your routine, they require less mental effort to complete. Start by incorporating small, positive habits into your daily life and gradually build on them.

3. **Monitor Your Progress:**
   Keeping track of your progress is essential for staying disciplined and consistent. Use a journal, app, or simple checklist to monitor your daily activities. Reflecting on your progress regularly can provide motivation and help you adjust your approach if necessary.

4. **Hold Yourself Accountable:**
   Accountability is key to maintaining discipline and consistency. Share your goals with someone you trust or join a group with similar objectives.

Having someone to check in with can provide the extra push you need to stay on track.

5. **Be Patient and Kind to Yourself:**
Developing discipline and consistency takes time, and setbacks are inevitable. It's important to be patient with yourself and not get discouraged by occasional lapses. Instead of giving up, view setbacks as learning opportunities and recommit to your goals.

Conclusion: The Synergy of Discipline and Consistency

Discipline and consistency are like two sides of the same coin—each complements and strengthens the other. Discipline helps you start the journey toward your goals, while consistency ensures you keep moving forward, even when the initial excitement fades. Together, they form a powerful combination that can lead to extraordinary achievements. By cultivating these qualities in your daily life, you set yourself up for success, not just in the short term, but for the long haul. Embrace discipline and consistency, and you'll find that the path to your dreams becomes clearer, more manageable, and ultimately, achievable.

Chapter 6: Overcoming Challenges

Dealing with Burnout

Burnout is a state of physical, emotional, and mental exhaustion caused by prolonged stress and overwork. It's more than just feeling tired or stressed; it's a deep sense of fatigue and disillusionment that can affect every aspect of your life. Burnout often creeps up gradually, making it difficult to recognize until you're deeply entrenched in its grip. Dealing with burnout effectively requires a comprehensive approach that addresses its causes, symptoms, and long-term prevention strategies. Here's how you can navigate and overcome burnout in a way that leads to sustained well-being and renewed energy.

Understanding Burnout

Burnout is a multifaceted issue that typically stems from chronic stress at work, but it can also be influenced by personal life challenges, lack of work-life balance, and insufficient self-care. It manifests in various ways, including physical exhaustion, emotional numbness, and a decrease in professional efficacy. Common signs of burnout include:

1. **Chronic Fatigue:**
   Feeling constantly drained, even after a full night's sleep, is a hallmark of burnout. This exhaustion can make it difficult to get through the day and diminish your ability to perform even simple tasks.

2. **Detachment and Cynicism:**
   Burnout often leads to a sense of detachment from work and colleagues. You may start feeling cynical about your job, losing interest in tasks you once enjoyed, and withdrawing from social interactions.

3. **Reduced Productivity:**
   As burnout progresses, it becomes harder to stay focused and productive. Tasks that once seemed manageable may now feel overwhelming, and your overall performance may decline.

4. **Physical Symptoms:**
   Burnout can also manifest physically, with symptoms like headaches, digestive issues, and insomnia. These physical signs are your body's way of signaling that it's under too much stress.

Immediate Steps to Address Burnout

If you're experiencing burnout, it's crucial to take immediate steps to alleviate the symptoms and begin the recovery process. Here's how you can start:

1. **Acknowledge the Problem:**
   The first step in dealing with burnout is recognizing and acknowledging it. Many people try to push through burnout, believing they can overcome it with sheer willpower. However, ignoring burnout only exacerbates the problem. Accept that you're experiencing burnout and that you need to take steps to address it.

2. **Take a Break:**
   When burnout is severe, taking a break from work is often necessary. Whether it's a short vacation, a weekend getaway, or simply a few days off, stepping away from your routine can give you the mental and physical rest you need. During this time, focus on activities that rejuvenate you—spending time in nature, engaging in hobbies, or simply resting.

3. **Seek Support:**
   Don't be afraid to ask for help. Talk to a trusted friend, family member, or therapist about what you're going through. Sometimes, just verbalizing your feelings can relieve some of the emotional burden. Additionally, consider speaking with your employer about your workload or any adjustments that could help reduce stress.

4. **Prioritize Self-Care:**
   Self-care is essential in combating burnout. This includes getting enough sleep, eating a balanced diet, and exercising regularly. Incorporate activities that promote relaxation and joy into your daily routine, whether it's reading, meditating, or spending time with loved ones. Self-care is not a luxury; it's a necessity for maintaining your well-being.

Long-Term Strategies for Preventing Burnout

Once you've addressed the immediate symptoms of burnout, it's important to implement long-term strategies to prevent it from recurring.

These strategies can help you create a more balanced and sustainable lifestyle:

1. **Set Boundaries:**
   One of the leading causes of burnout is a lack of boundaries between work and personal life. Set clear limits on your working hours and stick to them. Avoid checking work emails or taking calls outside of these hours. Communicate your boundaries to your employer and colleagues so they understand and respect your need for personal time.

2. **Practice Time Management:**
   Effective time management can help reduce the stress that leads to burnout. Prioritize your tasks based on importance and urgency, and delegate when possible. Break down large projects into smaller, manageable tasks to avoid feeling overwhelmed. Remember to schedule regular breaks throughout your day to rest and recharge.

3. **Cultivate a Support System:**
   Having a strong support system is crucial for preventing burnout. Build relationships with people who can provide emotional support and encouragement. Whether it's family, friends, or colleagues, having people you can turn to during challenging times can make a significant difference in your ability to cope with stress.

4. **Engage in Regular Reflection:**
   Regularly reflecting on your goals, values, and priorities can help you stay aligned with what truly matters to you. This reflection can prevent you from becoming overly absorbed in work and neglecting other important aspects of your life. Consider journaling or practicing mindfulness to stay connected with your inner self.

5. **Pursue Work-Life Balance:**
   Strive for a healthy balance between work and personal life. Engage in activities outside of work that bring you joy and fulfillment, such as hobbies, volunteering, or spending time with loved ones. A balanced life is key to maintaining long-term well-being and preventing burnout.

Conclusion: Reclaiming Your Energy and Passion

Burnout is a serious issue that can have profound effects on your physical and mental health, as well as your overall quality of life. By recognizing the signs of burnout and taking proactive steps to address it, you can regain your energy, passion, and enthusiasm for life. Remember that dealing with burnout is not a one-time fix, but an ongoing process that requires consistent effort and self-awareness. With the right strategies and support, you can overcome burnout and create a more balanced, fulfilling life that aligns with your true values and aspirations.

Staying Motivated

Staying motivated is one of the most important yet challenging aspects of achieving any goal, whether personal or professional. Motivation is the driving force that pushes you to take action, overcome obstacles, and persist through difficulties. However, maintaining a high level of motivation over time can be difficult, especially when faced with setbacks or monotony. Understanding how to sustain motivation can be a game-changer in your journey toward success. Here's a guide on how to stay motivated, even when the going gets tough.

Understand Your "Why"

The foundation of staying motivated is understanding your "why"—the reason behind your goals and actions. When you have a clear understanding of why you're pursuing something, it's easier to stay focused and driven. Your "why" gives your efforts meaning and purpose, making the journey more fulfilling.

1. **Define Your Purpose:**
   Take some time to reflect on why your goal is important to you. Is it to improve your career, enhance your well-being, or contribute to something bigger than yourself? Knowing the deeper purpose behind your actions can provide a powerful source of motivation, especially during challenging times.

2. **Visualize Success:**
   Visualization is a powerful tool to maintain motivation. Picture yourself achieving your goals—how it will feel, what it will look like, and the benefits it will bring. This mental image can serve as a constant reminder of what you're working toward, helping you stay focused and energized.

Break Down Your Goals

Large goals can be overwhelming, and this can drain your motivation. Breaking down your goals into smaller, manageable tasks can make them less daunting and easier to achieve. This approach allows you to celebrate small wins along the way, which can boost your motivation to keep going.

1. **Set Milestones:**
   Divide your main goal into smaller milestones, each with its own timeline and reward. This not only makes the overall goal more attainable but also gives you a sense of progress and accomplishment. Each milestone achieved reinforces your motivation to move on to the next one.

2. **Focus on Daily Habits:**
   Instead of fixating on the end goal, concentrate on the daily habits that will lead you there. For example, if your goal is to write a book, commit to writing a certain number of words each day. Consistent, small efforts build up over time and keep your motivation high by showing you that progress is being made.

Stay Positive and Resilient

Your mindset plays a crucial role in maintaining motivation. Adopting a positive attitude and cultivating resilience can help you navigate the ups and downs of your journey without losing your drive.

1. **Embrace Challenges:**
   Challenges and setbacks are inevitable, but they don't have to derail your motivation. Instead of seeing them as obstacles, view them as

opportunities to learn and grow. When you approach difficulties with a positive mindset, you're more likely to stay motivated and find solutions.

2. **Practice Gratitude:**

Gratitude can shift your focus from what's going wrong to what's going right. Regularly take time to acknowledge and appreciate your progress, the support you have, and the lessons you've learned. Gratitude can boost your mood and reinforce your commitment to your goals.

3. **Reward Yourself:**

Celebrate your achievements, no matter how small. Rewards can be powerful motivators. Whether it's treating yourself to something you enjoy or taking a break, recognizing your efforts can reinforce positive behavior and keep your motivation high.

Surround Yourself with Support

The people around you can significantly impact your motivation levels. Surrounding yourself with supportive and positive individuals can help you stay motivated, especially when you're feeling discouraged.

1. **Seek Accountability:**

Share your goals with someone you trust who can hold you accountable. This could be a friend, family member, or mentor. Knowing that someone else is aware of your goals and is cheering you on can provide an extra layer of motivation to stay on track.

2. **Join a Community:**

Being part of a community with similar goals can provide a sense of camaraderie and support. Whether it's a professional network, a fitness group, or an online forum, connecting with others who are on a similar journey can inspire and motivate you to keep going.

3. **Learn from Role Models:**

Look to those who have achieved what you aspire to. Learning from their experiences, challenges, and successes can provide valuable insights and motivate you to persevere. Role models can serve as a reminder that success is possible, even in the face of difficulties.

Stay Flexible and Adaptable

Staying motivated doesn't mean sticking rigidly to a plan, even when it's not working. Flexibility and adaptability are key to sustaining motivation over the long term.

1. **Reevaluate and Adjust:**
   Periodically review your progress and be open to adjusting your approach if necessary. If you're not seeing the results you want, it might be time to change your strategy. Flexibility allows you to stay motivated by ensuring that your efforts are aligned with your goals.

2. **Stay Open to New Ideas:**
   Sometimes, a fresh perspective or a new approach can reignite your motivation. Be willing to explore new methods, tools, or strategies that might help you achieve your goals more effectively. Staying open to change can keep your journey dynamic and exciting.

Conclusion: Motivation as a Journey

Staying motivated is a continuous process that requires effort, reflection, and adjustment. It's normal for motivation to fluctuate, but by understanding your "why," breaking down your goals, maintaining a positive mindset, seeking support, and staying adaptable, you can sustain your drive over the long haul. Remember that motivation is not just about reaching the end goal; it's about enjoying and learning from the journey itself. By cultivating these habits and mindsets, you can keep your motivation alive and well, propelling you toward success and fulfillment.

Managing Distractions and Interruptions

In today's fast-paced world, managing distractions and interruptions has become a critical skill for maintaining productivity and focus. Whether you're working on an important project, studying for an exam, or trying to complete daily tasks, distractions can quickly derail your progress and consume valuable time. From constant notifications on your phone to unplanned interruptions by colleagues or family members, distractions are everywhere. However, with the right strategies, you can minimize these interruptions and create an environment that supports deep focus and efficiency. Here's how to effectively manage distractions and interruptions to stay on track and achieve your goals.

Identify Your Distractions

The first step in managing distractions is to identify what's pulling your attention away from your tasks. Distractions can be both external and internal, and understanding what disrupts your focus is essential for developing strategies to combat them.

1. **External Distractions:**
   These are distractions that come from your environment, such as phone notifications, social media, background noise, or people interrupting you. External distractions are often the most obvious and can be reduced or eliminated with some planning and discipline.

2. **Internal Distractions:**
   Internal distractions stem from your thoughts, emotions, or physical state. These might include worrying about personal issues, daydreaming, feeling hungry, or being tired. Internal distractions can be more challenging to manage because they require you to address the underlying causes.

Create a Distraction-Free Environment

One of the most effective ways to manage distractions is by creating an environment that minimizes interruptions and promotes focus. This involves both physical and digital aspects of your workspace.

1. **Optimize Your Workspace:**
   Designate a specific area for focused work, whether it's a home office, a quiet corner of a room, or a spot in a library. Make sure your workspace is tidy, well-organized, and free from unnecessary clutter. A clean and organized space can help reduce visual distractions and create a calm atmosphere that supports concentration.

2. **Limit Digital Distractions:**
   Digital distractions are among the most pervasive, but they can be managed with some proactive steps. Start by turning off non-essential notifications on your phone, computer, and other devices. Consider using apps or tools that block distracting websites or limit your time on social media. If possible, set your devices to "Do Not Disturb" mode while you're working on important tasks.

3. **Establish Boundaries:**
   If you're working from home or in a shared space, it's important to communicate your need for uninterrupted time. Let family members or roommates know when you're focusing and request that they minimize interruptions during those periods. In a workplace setting, you can use visual cues like wearing headphones or closing your office door to signal that you're in deep work mode.

Develop Focus-Enhancing Habits

In addition to creating a distraction-free environment, developing habits that enhance your focus and reduce the likelihood of interruptions is crucial for maintaining productivity.

1. **Practice Time Blocking:**
   Time blocking is a powerful technique for managing your schedule and reducing distractions. By dedicating specific blocks of time to particular

tasks, you can concentrate fully on one thing at a time without the need to multitask. During these blocks, commit to focusing solely on the task at hand, and avoid switching to other activities until the time block is over.

2. **Use the Pomodoro Technique:**
The Pomodoro Technique involves working for 25 minutes (a "Pomodoro") followed by a 5-minute break. After four Pomodoros, take a longer break of 15-30 minutes. This method can help you maintain focus while also giving your mind regular intervals of rest, reducing the risk of burnout. The frequent breaks also allow you to address minor distractions without losing overall momentum.

3. **Prioritize Your Tasks:**
Not all tasks are equally important. Prioritize your to-do list by focusing on high-impact activities first. By tackling the most critical tasks when your energy and focus are at their peak, you ensure that even if interruptions occur later in the day, the most important work is already done.

4. **Mindfulness and Meditation:**
Practicing mindfulness and meditation can help you develop greater control over your attention and reduce the impact of internal distractions. Regular meditation trains your mind to stay focused on the present moment, making it easier to return to your task when your mind starts to wander.

Handle Interruptions with Grace

Despite your best efforts, interruptions are sometimes unavoidable. Learning how to manage them effectively without losing your focus is key to staying productive.

1. **Set Expectations:**
When possible, set expectations with those around you about when you're available and when you're not. For example, let colleagues know that you're available for questions between certain hours, but need

focused time during others. Clear communication can significantly reduce unnecessary interruptions.

2. **Use the "Two-Minute Rule":**
   If an interruption is brief and can be handled in two minutes or less, address it quickly and then return to your task. This approach prevents minor distractions from lingering and allows you to get back to your work with minimal disruption.

3. **Politely Deflect:**
   If you're in the middle of focused work and someone interrupts, it's okay to politely ask if you can address their issue later. For example, you might say, "I'm in the middle of something important right now. Can we discuss this in an hour?" Most people will understand and respect your need for uninterrupted time.

4. **Stay Calm and Refocus:**
   When interruptions do occur, it's important to stay calm and not let them frustrate you. After handling the interruption, take a moment to refocus before diving back into your task. A few deep breaths or a quick stretch can help you regain your concentration.

Conclusion: Mastering Distractions for Better Focus

Managing distractions and interruptions is a skill that can significantly enhance your productivity and overall well-being. By creating a distraction-free environment, developing focus-enhancing habits, and learning to handle interruptions with grace, you can maintain the deep focus needed to achieve your goals. Remember that managing distractions is an ongoing process that requires regular adjustments and self-awareness. With practice, you can build a routine that minimizes disruptions and allows you to work more efficiently and effectively, leading to greater satisfaction and success in your endeavors.

Chapter 7: Productivity in Different Contexts

Productivity at Work

In today's competitive world, productivity at work isn't just about getting more done—it's about getting the right things done efficiently. High productivity means making the most of your time, energy, and resources to achieve your goals and contribute meaningfully to your organization. However, staying productive in the workplace can be challenging due to constant distractions, competing priorities, and the pressure to perform. Here's how you can enhance your productivity at work and make each day more effective and fulfilling.

Understand and Set Clear Goals

One of the key elements of workplace productivity is having a clear understanding of what you need to achieve. Without clear goals, it's easy to get sidetracked or spend time on tasks that don't contribute to your overall objectives.

1. **Set SMART Goals:**
    SMART goals—Specific, Measurable, Achievable, Relevant, and Time-bound—provide a clear framework for what you need to accomplish. For example, instead of setting a vague goal like "improve sales," a SMART goal would be "increase sales by 10% in the next quarter by focusing on upselling to existing clients." This clarity helps you stay focused and measure your progress.

2. **Prioritize Tasks:**
    Not all tasks are equally important. Use prioritization techniques like the Eisenhower Matrix, which categorizes tasks into four quadrants:

urgent and important, important but not urgent, urgent but not important, and neither urgent nor important. Focus on tasks that are both urgent and important, and schedule time for important but not urgent tasks to prevent them from becoming urgent.

Optimize Your Workflow

Once you've set clear goals and prioritized your tasks, the next step is to optimize your workflow to maximize efficiency. This involves organizing your workday and adopting strategies that help you stay on track.

1. **Time Blocking:**
   Time blocking is a technique where you schedule your day into blocks of time dedicated to specific tasks or activities. For example, you might block out 9:00 AM to 11:00 AM for focused work on a project, followed by a 30-minute block for responding to emails. This method helps you manage your time more effectively and ensures that important tasks get the attention they deserve.

2. **Batch Similar Tasks:**
   Grouping similar tasks together, known as task batching, can save you time and mental energy. For instance, instead of responding to emails throughout the day, set aside specific times to handle all your email correspondence. Similarly, you can batch tasks like making phone calls or doing administrative work. This reduces the cognitive load associated with constantly switching between different types of tasks.

3. **Use Productivity Tools:**
   There are numerous productivity tools and apps designed to help you manage your tasks, time, and projects more effectively. Tools like Trello, Asana, or Microsoft To-Do can help you organize your tasks, set deadlines, and track progress. Additionally, time-tracking apps like Toggl can give you insights into how you're spending your time, allowing you to make adjustments for better efficiency.

Manage Your Energy

Productivity isn't just about managing your time; it's also about managing your energy. Even if you have plenty of time, you won't be productive if you're mentally or physically drained. To stay productive, it's important to pay attention to your energy levels throughout the day and adjust your work accordingly.

1. **Identify Peak Energy Times:**
   Everyone has certain times of the day when they're most alert and focused. For some, it's early in the morning; for others, it might be in the afternoon or evening. Identify your peak energy times and schedule your most important or challenging tasks during these periods. This ensures that you're working on high-priority tasks when you're at your best.

2. **Take Regular Breaks:**
   Working for long periods without breaks can lead to burnout and reduced productivity. The Pomodoro Technique, which involves working for 25 minutes followed by a 5-minute break, is an effective way to maintain focus while preventing mental fatigue. Longer breaks of 15-30 minutes after every few hours of work can also help you recharge and come back to your tasks with renewed energy.

3. **Stay Physically Active:**
   Physical activity is crucial for maintaining energy levels and mental clarity. Even short bursts of exercise, such as a quick walk or stretching exercises, can boost your mood and energy. Additionally, staying hydrated and eating nutritious meals can support sustained energy throughout the day.

Cultivate a Productive Mindset

A productive mindset is essential for maintaining long-term productivity. This involves cultivating habits and attitudes that support focus, resilience, and continuous improvement.

1. **Embrace Continuous Learning:**
   Staying productive at work often requires adapting to new tools, techniques, and knowledge. Embrace a mindset of continuous learning by regularly seeking out opportunities for professional development. This

could involve taking online courses, attending workshops, or simply staying updated on industry trends. A commitment to learning keeps your skills sharp and your mind engaged.

2. **Practice Mindfulness:**
   Mindfulness involves being fully present and engaged in whatever you're doing. By practicing mindfulness, you can reduce stress, improve focus, and enhance your ability to handle complex tasks. Simple mindfulness exercises, such as deep breathing or a few minutes of meditation, can help you stay calm and focused throughout the day.

3. **Reflect and Adjust:**
   At the end of each day or week, take time to reflect on what went well and what could be improved. This reflection helps you identify patterns in your productivity and make adjustments as needed. Whether it's tweaking your schedule, trying a new productivity tool, or adjusting your goals, regular reflection ensures that you're constantly improving your work habits.

Conclusion: Achieving Sustainable Productivity

Productivity at work isn't about working harder; it's about working smarter. By setting clear goals, optimizing your workflow, managing your energy, and cultivating a productive mindset, you can achieve sustainable productivity that not only helps you meet your objectives but also enhances your overall job satisfaction. Remember, productivity is a journey, not a destination. Continuously refine your approach, stay flexible, and adapt to the changing demands of your work environment to maintain high levels of productivity and achieve long-term success.

Managing Home and Personal Life

Balancing home and personal life can be challenging, especially in a world that often demands more of our time and energy. Whether you're juggling work, family, personal goals, or social obligations, finding a harmonious balance is essential for your overall well-being and happiness. Successfully managing home and personal life requires planning, prioritization, and a focus on what truly matters. Here's how you can effectively manage these aspects of your life to create a fulfilling and balanced existence.

Set Priorities and Define What Matters Most

One of the first steps in managing home and personal life is to clearly define your priorities. What are the most important aspects of your life that you want to focus on? These might include your family, personal health, career, friendships, or hobbies. Once you have a clear understanding of your priorities, you can make decisions that align with these values.

1. **Identify Your Core Values:**
   Take time to reflect on what truly matters to you. Are your relationships your top priority? Is maintaining a healthy lifestyle essential to your well-being? By identifying your core values, you can make more informed choices about how to allocate your time and energy.

2. **Set Realistic Goals:**
   Break down your priorities into specific, achievable goals. For example, if spending quality time with family is important, set a goal to have dinner together at least three times a week. If personal health is a priority, aim to exercise for 30 minutes daily. Realistic goals help you stay focused and motivated without becoming overwhelmed.

3. **Create a Vision for Your Life:**
   Envision how you want your life to look in different areas, such as home, work, health, and relationships. This vision serves as a guidepost, helping you make choices that support your long-term happiness and fulfillment.

Create a Balanced Routine

A balanced routine is the foundation of effectively managing home and personal life. A well-structured routine helps you allocate time for various activities while ensuring that no single aspect of your life dominates the others.

1. **Designate Time for Each Aspect:**
   Allocate specific times in your day or week for work, family, self-care, and other important activities. For example, you might reserve mornings for personal fitness, afternoons for work tasks, and evenings for family time. By creating a routine that includes all areas of your life, you ensure that nothing gets neglected.

2. **Use Time Management Techniques:**
   Time management techniques like time blocking or the Pomodoro Technique can help you stay organized and focused. For instance, you can block off time for household chores, hobbies, or relaxation. These techniques prevent you from overcommitting to one area and allow you to switch between different activities efficiently.

3. **Be Flexible:**
   While having a routine is important, it's equally important to remain flexible. Life is unpredictable, and there will be times when your routine needs to be adjusted. Whether it's a family emergency, an unexpected work deadline, or simply needing a break, being adaptable ensures that you can handle disruptions without feeling stressed or overwhelmed.

Practice Self-Care and Mindfulness

Taking care of yourself is crucial for managing both home and personal life. When you prioritize self-care, you're better equipped to handle life's demands and maintain a positive outlook.

1. **Prioritize Your Health:**
   Your physical and mental health should be a top priority. Ensure that you're getting enough sleep, eating a balanced diet, and engaging in regular physical activity. Exercise not only improves your physical health but also reduces stress and boosts your mood.

2. **Practice Mindfulness:**

Mindfulness is the practice of being present in the moment without judgment. It can help you stay calm and focused, especially when life gets hectic. Simple mindfulness exercises, like deep breathing, meditation, or mindful walking, can be integrated into your daily routine to reduce stress and increase your awareness.

3. **Set Boundaries:**
Establishing boundaries is essential for maintaining balance. Learn to say no to commitments that don't align with your priorities or that could overwhelm you. Setting boundaries also means carving out time for yourself, even if it's just a few minutes of quiet time each day.

Foster Positive Relationships

Healthy relationships are a key component of a fulfilling life. Whether it's with family, friends, or colleagues, nurturing positive connections can enhance your sense of belonging and support your overall well-being.

1. **Communicate Openly:**
Effective communication is the foundation of strong relationships. Be honest about your needs, listen actively, and show empathy towards others. Open communication helps prevent misunderstandings and strengthens your bonds with loved ones.

2. **Make Time for Loved Ones:**
No matter how busy you are, it's important to make time for the people who matter most. Whether it's having regular family dinners, scheduling coffee dates with friends, or simply checking in with loved ones, these interactions are vital for maintaining strong, supportive relationships.

3. **Show Appreciation:**
Expressing gratitude and appreciation can deepen your relationships and create a positive atmosphere at home. A simple thank you, a kind gesture, or acknowledging someone's efforts can go a long way in fostering goodwill and mutual respect.

Balance Responsibilities and Leisure

Balancing responsibilities with leisure activities is essential for maintaining a healthy work-life balance. While it's important to fulfill your duties, it's equally important to make time for relaxation and fun.

1. **Delegate and Share Responsibilities:**
   Don't hesitate to delegate tasks or share responsibilities with others. Whether it's household chores, work assignments, or community obligations, sharing the load can prevent burnout and create a more balanced life.

2. **Schedule Leisure Activities:**
   Make time for activities that bring you joy and relaxation. Whether it's reading, watching movies, gardening, or pursuing a hobby, leisure activities provide a necessary break from the demands of daily life and help you recharge.

3. **Unplug and Unwind:**
   In our digital age, it's easy to become overwhelmed by constant connectivity. Set aside time to unplug from devices and enjoy activities that don't involve screens. This could be spending time in nature, enjoying a meal with family, or simply being present in the moment.

Conclusion: Creating Harmony in Your Life

Managing home and personal life requires a thoughtful approach that prioritizes what truly matters, creates balance, and nurtures well-being. By setting clear priorities, developing a balanced routine, practicing self-care, fostering positive relationships, and balancing responsibilities with leisure, you can create a harmonious life that supports your happiness and fulfillment. Remember that balance is not a one-time achievement but an ongoing process that requires regular adjustments and self-awareness. With dedication and mindfulness, you can build a life that feels both productive and rewarding.

Remote Work Productivity

Remote work has become increasingly common, offering flexibility and freedom that many employees value. However, working from home or any location outside a traditional office comes with its unique challenges. Productivity in a remote work environment requires a different set of strategies compared to working in a conventional office setting. To thrive in remote work, it's crucial to establish routines, maintain focus, and create a work-life balance that keeps you both productive and satisfied. Here's how you can maximize your productivity while working remotely.

Establish a Dedicated Workspace

One of the first steps to staying productive while working remotely is to create a dedicated workspace. This space doesn't necessarily have to be an entire room, but it should be an area where you can focus solely on work.

1. **Choose the Right Location:**
   Select a spot in your home that is quiet, comfortable, and free from distractions. It's important that this space feels separate from the areas you use for relaxation, like your living room or bedroom. This physical separation helps reinforce the mental distinction between work and leisure.

2. **Invest in the Right Equipment:**
   Equip your workspace with the tools you need to work efficiently. This might include a comfortable chair, a desk, a computer with a reliable internet connection, and any other tools specific to your job. Proper ergonomics are crucial, so ensure your setup is comfortable and supports good posture.

3. **Personalize Your Workspace:**
   Adding personal touches like plants, artwork, or motivational quotes can make your workspace more inviting. A well-organized and pleasant environment can boost your mood and, in turn, your productivity.

Create a Structured Routine

Without the structure of a traditional office environment, it's easy to let your day slip away. Establishing a routine is essential to staying on track and ensuring that your workday is both productive and efficient.

1. **Set Regular Working Hours:**
    Try to stick to a consistent schedule, just as you would in an office. Set specific start and end times for your workday, and take regular breaks to prevent burnout. A consistent routine helps you maintain a work-life balance and makes it easier for others to know when you're available.

2. **Prioritize Your Tasks:**
    Start each day by planning out your tasks. Use a to-do list or a digital task manager to prioritize your work. Tackle the most important or challenging tasks first, when your energy and focus are at their peak. This approach, often referred to as "eating the frog," helps you build momentum and ensures that critical tasks get done.

3. **Incorporate Breaks and Movement:**
    Sitting at a desk for long periods can lead to fatigue and decreased productivity. Incorporate short breaks into your routine, such as the Pomodoro Technique, where you work for 25 minutes and then take a 5-minute break. Use these breaks to stand up, stretch, or take a quick walk. Physical activity can refresh your mind and prevent burnout.

Minimize Distractions

Remote work often presents more distractions than a traditional office environment. Whether it's household chores, social media, or family members, it's important to manage these distractions to maintain productivity.

1. **Set Boundaries:**
    Communicate with the people you live with about your work schedule and the importance of minimizing interruptions during work hours. Establishing clear boundaries helps others understand when you are and aren't available.

2. **Limit Digital Distractions:**
   The internet can be a major source of distraction. Consider using apps or browser extensions that block distracting websites during work hours. Tools like Focus@Will or background music designed to enhance focus can also help you stay on task.

3. **Manage Notifications:**
   Turn off non-essential notifications on your devices during work hours. Constant pings from your phone or computer can disrupt your focus and make it harder to complete tasks. Instead, check emails and messages at scheduled intervals to stay on top of communication without letting it dominate your day.

Stay Connected and Engaged

One of the challenges of remote work is the potential for isolation. Staying connected with your team and maintaining a sense of engagement is crucial for both productivity and morale.

1. **Regular Check-ins:**
   Schedule regular check-ins with your team or manager. These can be daily stand-ups, weekly meetings, or informal chats. Regular communication helps keep everyone aligned and provides opportunities to discuss any challenges or roadblocks.

2. **Use Collaboration Tools:**
   Utilize digital tools that facilitate communication and collaboration, such as Slack, Microsoft Teams, or Zoom. These tools help you stay connected with colleagues, share ideas, and collaborate on projects, even when working from different locations.

3. **Participate in Virtual Social Activities:**
   Many companies offer virtual social activities, such as online coffee breaks, team-building games, or virtual happy hours. Participating in these activities can help you feel more connected to your coworkers and maintain a sense of camaraderie.

Balance Work and Life

One of the key benefits of remote work is the potential for better work-life balance. However, without clear boundaries, work can easily spill over into personal time, leading to burnout.

1. **Set Clear Work-Life Boundaries:**
   At the end of your workday, make a clear transition from work to personal time. This could be as simple as closing your laptop, turning off work-related notifications, or engaging in a post-work ritual, like going for a walk. Clear boundaries help you fully disconnect from work and recharge.

2. **Take Advantage of Flexibility:**
   Remote work often offers more flexibility in how you structure your day. Use this to your advantage by scheduling work around your most productive times or by taking breaks when you need them. Flexibility can help you achieve a better balance between work and personal life.

3. **Prioritize Self-Care:**
   Make time for activities that nurture your physical and mental well-being. Whether it's exercising, pursuing hobbies, or spending time with loved ones, self-care is essential for maintaining long-term productivity and preventing burnout.

Conclusion: Thriving in a Remote Work Environment

Remote work offers incredible opportunities for flexibility and autonomy, but it also requires a proactive approach to maintain productivity. By creating a dedicated workspace, establishing a structured routine, minimizing distractions, staying connected, and balancing work and life, you can thrive in a remote work environment. Remember, productivity isn't just about getting more done—it's about working smarter, maintaining well-being, and finding a balance that works for you. With the right strategies, you can enjoy the benefits of remote work while achieving your professional goals.

Chapter 8: Continuous Improvement

Reviewing and Reflecting on Your Progress

Reviewing and reflecting on your progress is an essential practice for personal and professional growth. It allows you to assess where you stand in relation to your goals, understand what's working, and identify areas that need improvement. Regular reflection helps you stay aligned with your objectives, boosts motivation, and ensures continuous progress. Here's how you can effectively review and reflect on your progress to ensure you're on the right path and making meaningful strides toward your goals.

Why Reviewing and Reflecting is Important

Reviewing and reflecting are not just about looking back on what you've done; it's about understanding the why and how behind your actions. This process enables you to:

1. **Gain Clarity on Your Progress:**
    By regularly reviewing your work or personal goals, you gain a clearer picture of how much progress you've made. This helps you see whether you're on track or if adjustments are needed to meet your objectives.

2. **Identify Strengths and Weaknesses:**
    Reflection allows you to recognize what you're doing well and where you might be struggling. Understanding your strengths can help you

leverage them further, while acknowledging weaknesses provides an opportunity to develop or seek assistance in those areas.

3. **Stay Motivated:**
   Seeing tangible progress, even if it's small, can be incredibly motivating. Regular reflection helps you celebrate your wins, no matter how minor, and keeps you motivated to continue pushing forward.

4. **Make Informed Decisions:**
   Reflecting on past actions and decisions gives you insights into what works and what doesn't. This knowledge is invaluable for making more informed decisions in the future, leading to better outcomes.

How to Effectively Review Your Progress

Reviewing your progress involves taking a step back to assess what you've accomplished and how you've done it. This process can be broken down into several steps:

1. **Set Regular Review Intervals:**
   Schedule regular times to review your progress, whether it's daily, weekly, or monthly. Consistency is key to staying on top of your goals and making timely adjustments. A weekly review, for example, can help you reflect on the past week's achievements and challenges, setting you up for success in the coming week.

2. **Use Metrics and Data:**
   Whenever possible, use specific metrics to measure your progress. These could be quantitative, like the number of tasks completed or sales made, or qualitative, such as feedback received or personal satisfaction levels. Data-driven reviews provide objective insights that can guide your next steps.

3. **Compare with Your Goals:**
   Revisit the goals you set for yourself and compare them with your current progress. Are you where you expected to be at this point? If not, analyze why that might be the case. This comparison helps you gauge your effectiveness and whether your strategies are working.

4. **Document Your Findings:**
   Keep a record of your reviews. Writing down your thoughts, observations, and insights helps solidify your learning and provides a reference for future reflection. Over time, this documentation can reveal patterns and trends that are crucial for long-term growth.

Reflecting on Your Progress

Reflection goes beyond merely reviewing your progress; it involves deeper introspection into your experiences, emotions, and thought processes. Here's how to reflect effectively:

1. **Ask Reflective Questions:**
   Engage in self-questioning to gain insights into your actions and outcomes. Some helpful questions include:
   - What did I do well this week/month?
   - What challenges did I face, and how did I handle them?
   - What could I have done differently?
   - How did my actions align with my values and goals?
   - What lessons have I learned, and how can I apply them moving forward?

2. **Consider Both Successes and Failures:**
   Reflection should include both your successes and your setbacks. While it's important to celebrate your wins, it's equally crucial to learn from your mistakes. Reflecting on failures without judgment allows you to grow and avoid repeating the same errors.

3. **Connect Reflection to Future Action:**
   The purpose of reflection is not just to look back, but to inform your future actions. Use the insights gained from reflection to adjust your plans, set new goals, or modify your approach. This continuous loop of action, review, and reflection is key to sustained progress.

4. **Practice Gratitude and Self-Compassion:**
   While reflecting, practice gratitude for the progress you've made and the opportunities you've had. Also, be kind to yourself, especially when

things don't go as planned. Self-compassion helps you maintain a positive mindset, which is crucial for long-term success.

Tools for Reviewing and Reflecting

Several tools can assist you in reviewing and reflecting on your progress:

1. **Journaling:**
   Keeping a journal is one of the most effective ways to reflect. Writing about your experiences, thoughts, and feelings allows you to process them deeply. You can also revisit your journal entries later to track your growth over time.

2. **Progress Tracking Apps:**
   There are many digital tools designed to help you track your progress toward goals. Apps like Trello, Asana, or even simple spreadsheets can provide visual representations of your progress, making it easier to review and reflect.

3. **Feedback from Others:**
   Sometimes, outside perspectives can provide valuable insights that you might overlook. Seek feedback from mentors, peers, or colleagues to gain a more well-rounded view of your progress.

Conclusion: The Power of Continuous Improvement

Reviewing and reflecting on your progress is a powerful practice that drives continuous improvement. By regularly assessing your achievements and setbacks, you can stay aligned with your goals, learn from your experiences, and make informed decisions that propel you forward. Remember, progress is not always linear, and it's okay to adjust your course as needed. What's important is that you stay committed to your growth and use reflection as a tool to guide your journey. With consistent review and reflection, you'll find yourself steadily moving closer to your goals, equipped with the knowledge and insights to overcome any obstacles along the way.

Adapting and Evolving Your Strategies

In a rapidly changing world, the ability to adapt and evolve your strategies is crucial for both personal and professional success. Whether you're pursuing long-term goals, managing a business, or navigating life's unpredictable twists and turns, being flexible and willing to change your approach can make all the difference. The most successful individuals and organizations are those that continuously assess their strategies, make necessary adjustments, and evolve to meet new challenges and opportunities. Here's how you can master the art of adaptation and ensure your strategies remain effective and relevant.

The Importance of Adaptability

Adaptability is the capacity to adjust your actions, thoughts, and behaviors in response to changing circumstances. In today's fast-paced environment, where technology, markets, and social dynamics are constantly evolving, being rigid can lead to stagnation. Here's why adaptability is essential:

1. **Responding to Change:**
   The world is unpredictable, and unexpected changes can occur at any time. Whether it's a shift in market conditions, new technology, or a personal life event, being adaptable allows you to respond quickly and effectively. Instead of being thrown off course, you can pivot and continue moving forward.

2. **Seizing New Opportunities:**
   Opportunities often arise from change. By staying adaptable, you can recognize and capitalize on these opportunities. This might mean altering your business model, learning a new skill, or exploring a different career path. Being open to change increases your chances of success.

3. **Overcoming Obstacles:**

No strategy is foolproof, and challenges are inevitable. Adaptability enables you to navigate these obstacles without losing sight of your goals. Instead of getting stuck when things don't go as planned, you can find alternative solutions and keep progressing.

How to Adapt and Evolve Your Strategies

Adapting and evolving your strategies is a continuous process that involves reflection, learning, and action. Here are steps you can take to ensure your strategies remain effective:

1. **Regularly Assess Your Strategies:**
   Just because something worked in the past doesn't mean it will always be effective. Regularly assess your strategies to ensure they're still aligned with your goals and the current environment. This involves reviewing your progress, gathering feedback, and staying informed about relevant trends and developments.

2. **Embrace a Growth Mindset:**
   A growth mindset is the belief that you can develop your abilities and intelligence through effort, learning, and persistence. This mindset encourages you to view challenges as opportunities to grow rather than as setbacks. With a growth mindset, you're more likely to adapt your strategies when necessary and continuously evolve.

3. **Stay Informed and Anticipate Change:**
   Keep yourself informed about industry trends, technological advancements, and other factors that could impact your strategies. By anticipating change, you can prepare in advance and make proactive adjustments. This might involve investing in new tools, learning new skills, or adjusting your long-term plans.

4. **Experiment and Innovate:**
   Don't be afraid to experiment with new approaches. Innovation often comes from trying out different ideas and seeing what works. If a particular strategy isn't yielding the desired results, explore alternative methods. Even small changes can lead to significant improvements.

5. **Learn from Success and Failure:**
   Both success and failure provide valuable learning experiences. When a strategy works well, analyze why it was successful and consider how you can replicate or build on that success. When a strategy fails, don't be discouraged—use it as an opportunity to learn. Understanding what didn't work and why can help you refine your approach and avoid similar pitfalls in the future.

6. **Be Open to Feedback:**
   Feedback from others can offer new perspectives and insights that you might not have considered. Whether it's from colleagues, mentors, customers, or friends, constructive feedback can help you identify areas for improvement and opportunities to adapt your strategies. Be open to suggestions and willing to make changes based on the feedback you receive.

7. **Balance Consistency with Flexibility:**
   While adaptability is crucial, it's also important to maintain consistency in your core values and long-term vision. The key is to be flexible in your methods while staying true to your overarching goals. This balance allows you to evolve without losing sight of what matters most.

Overcoming the Challenges of Adaptation

Adapting and evolving your strategies isn't always easy. It can be challenging to let go of methods that you're comfortable with or that have worked in the past. Here are some tips to overcome these challenges:

1. **Manage Fear of Change:**
   Change can be intimidating, but it's often necessary for growth. Acknowledge any fears or uncertainties you may have and remind yourself of the potential benefits of adapting your strategies. Focus on the positive outcomes that can come from change rather than the discomfort of the process.

2. **Avoid Overthinking:**
   While it's important to thoughtfully consider your strategies, overthinking can lead to paralysis by analysis. Don't get so caught up in

analyzing every detail that you hesitate to take action. Sometimes, you need to take a leap of faith and make adjustments as you go.

3. **Cultivate Resilience:**
   Adaptation requires resilience—the ability to bounce back from setbacks and keep moving forward. Cultivate resilience by staying optimistic, learning from your experiences, and maintaining a strong support system. Resilience will help you navigate the ups and downs of adapting your strategies.

Conclusion: The Path to Continuous Growth

Adapting and evolving your strategies is an ongoing journey that requires self-awareness, flexibility, and a willingness to embrace change. By regularly assessing your strategies, staying open to new ideas, and learning from your experiences, you can ensure that your approaches remain effective in achieving your goals. Remember, success in today's world isn't just about sticking to a plan—it's about being able to pivot, innovate, and grow in response to the ever-changing landscape. Embrace the process of adaptation, and you'll find yourself better equipped to navigate challenges, seize opportunities, and achieve long-term success.

Lifelong Learning and Growth

Lifelong learning is the continuous, self-motivated pursuit of knowledge and skills throughout an individual's life. It goes beyond formal education and extends into everyday experiences, personal development, and professional growth. In a world where technology, industries, and societal norms are constantly evolving, the importance of lifelong learning cannot be overstated. Embracing this mindset can lead to a richer, more fulfilling life, both personally and professionally. Here's why lifelong learning is essential and how you can make it a core part of your life.

Why Lifelong Learning Matters

1. **Adapting to Change:**
   The world is in a constant state of flux, with new technologies, methodologies, and ideas emerging all the time. Lifelong learning enables you to stay current and relevant, ensuring that you can adapt to changes in your personal life, career, and society. Whether it's learning a new language, mastering a new software tool, or understanding a new cultural trend, being a lifelong learner equips you with the flexibility to navigate change with confidence.

2. **Enhancing Professional Competence:**
   In the professional realm, industries are rapidly evolving, and the skills required to succeed are constantly shifting. Lifelong learning helps you stay competitive in your career by continuously updating your skill set. It can lead to career advancement, better job opportunities, and the ability to take on new and challenging roles. Employers value individuals who are committed to self-improvement and who can bring fresh ideas and expertise to the table.

3. **Personal Growth and Fulfillment:**
   Lifelong learning is not just about professional success; it's also about personal growth and satisfaction. Engaging in new learning experiences can boost your confidence, improve your mental well-being, and give you a sense of accomplishment. Whether it's picking up a new hobby, exploring a different culture, or delving into a subject that interests you, lifelong learning adds depth and richness to your life.

4. **Fostering Creativity and Innovation:**
   Lifelong learning encourages you to think critically, explore new perspectives, and challenge existing paradigms. This mindset fosters creativity and innovation, as you are constantly exposed to new ideas and ways of thinking. By continuously learning, you can connect the dots between different fields of knowledge, leading to innovative solutions to complex problems.

5. **Building Resilience:**

Learning new skills and acquiring knowledge helps build resilience. When you're committed to lifelong learning, you're better equipped to handle life's challenges because you've developed a broad range of skills and a flexible mindset. This resilience allows you to bounce back from setbacks and view challenges as opportunities for growth rather than as obstacles.

How to Embrace Lifelong Learning

Lifelong learning is a mindset that anyone can adopt, regardless of age or background. Here are some practical ways to incorporate lifelong learning into your life:

1. **Set Learning Goals:**
   Just as you set goals for your career or personal life, it's important to set goals for your learning journey. Identify areas you're interested in or skills you'd like to develop, and set specific, measurable goals. For example, you might aim to read a certain number of books each year, complete an online course, or learn a new language within a specific timeframe.

2. **Explore Different Learning Methods:**
   Lifelong learning doesn't have to be confined to formal education. Explore different methods of learning that suit your lifestyle and preferences. This could include online courses, podcasts, workshops, reading books, attending seminars, or engaging in discussions with others. The key is to find learning methods that are enjoyable and effective for you.

3. **Stay Curious:**
   Cultivate a sense of curiosity about the world around you. Ask questions, seek out new experiences, and be open to exploring topics that are outside your usual areas of interest. Curiosity is the driving force behind lifelong learning, as it motivates you to discover and understand more about the world.

4. **Make Learning a Habit:**

Incorporate learning into your daily routine. This could be as simple as dedicating time each day to read, watch educational videos, or practice a new skill. By making learning a regular habit, it becomes a natural and enjoyable part of your life.

5. **Join Learning Communities:**
Surround yourself with like-minded individuals who value learning and personal growth. Join groups, forums, or communities where you can share knowledge, discuss ideas, and learn from others. Being part of a learning community provides support, motivation, and opportunities to expand your horizons.

6. **Reflect on Your Learning Journey:**
Take time to reflect on what you've learned and how it has impacted your life. Reflection helps solidify your learning, reinforces your progress, and allows you to identify areas where you can continue to grow. Keep a learning journal, where you can document your experiences, insights, and goals.

Overcoming Challenges in Lifelong Learning

While lifelong learning is incredibly rewarding, it can also come with challenges. Here's how to overcome some common obstacles:

1. **Time Management:**
Finding time for learning can be difficult, especially with a busy schedule. Prioritize learning by setting aside specific times each week dedicated to personal development. Even short, consistent periods of learning can add up over time.

2. **Information Overload:**
In the digital age, there's an overwhelming amount of information available, which can be daunting. Focus on quality over quantity by selecting reputable sources and setting clear learning objectives. This helps you stay focused and avoid getting lost in a sea of information.

3. **Staying Motivated:**

Maintaining motivation for lifelong learning can be challenging, especially when progress feels slow. Keep your learning goals visible, celebrate small wins, and remind yourself of the long-term benefits of continuous growth.

Conclusion: The Journey of Lifelong Growth

Lifelong learning is a journey, not a destination. It's about embracing the process of continuous growth, staying curious, and being open to new experiences. By committing to lifelong learning, you not only enhance your personal and professional life but also contribute to a more knowledgeable and innovative society. Remember, it's never too late to start learning, and the pursuit of knowledge is a lifelong adventure that enriches your life in countless ways.

Conclusion

Recap of Key Points

As we come to the conclusion of this journey into productivity, it's essential to take a moment to reflect on the key points covered. This recap will not only help solidify the ideas we've discussed but also serve as a reminder of the practical strategies that you can implement in your daily life. Here's a summary of the main concepts that will enhance your productivity, both personally and professionally.

1. **The Importance of Productivity**

Productivity is more than just getting things done—it's about doing the right things efficiently and effectively. Understanding why productivity matters is crucial because it impacts all aspects of your life. From your career to your personal development, being productive allows you to achieve your goals, reduce stress, and find a better balance between work and life. Remember, it's not just about working hard but working smart.

2. **The Science of Productivity**

Productivity is grounded in science. Understanding how our brain works, how habits form, and how motivation operates can help you make more informed decisions about your routines and work habits. By leveraging techniques like time management, focused work periods (such as the Pomodoro Technique), and avoiding multitasking, you can optimize your mental energy and maximize output without burning out.

3. **Setting SMART Goals**

One of the foundational principles of productivity is setting SMART goals—Specific, Measurable, Achievable, Relevant, and Time-bound. This framework helps you create clear and actionable goals that are realistic and trackable. By breaking down large objectives into smaller, manageable tasks, you can maintain momentum and see continuous progress toward your long-term vision.

4. **Prioritization and Time Management**

Prioritizing your tasks is essential for productivity. Not every task is equally important, and learning how to identify high-impact tasks can significantly boost your effectiveness. Using tools like the Eisenhower Matrix or the ABCDE Method, you can categorize your tasks and focus on what truly matters. Additionally, time management techniques such as time blocking and scheduling ensure that you allocate appropriate time for each task without feeling overwhelmed.

5. **Overcoming Procrastination**

Procrastination is one of the biggest roadblocks to productivity. We often delay tasks due to fear of failure, lack of motivation, or simply feeling overwhelmed. However, overcoming procrastination is possible by breaking tasks into smaller, more manageable steps, setting clear deadlines, and creating accountability. Cultivating self-discipline and using rewards to stay motivated are also effective ways to beat procrastination.

6. **Productivity Tools and Apps**

Leveraging modern productivity tools can streamline your workflow and help you stay organized. From task management systems like Trello or Asana to productivity apps like Todoist or Notion, there are countless options to fit your specific needs. These tools not only keep your tasks in check but also allow you to monitor your progress and adjust your strategies as needed.

7. **Building Productive Habits**

Habits are the foundation of long-term productivity. Establishing productive routines, such as morning and evening rituals, helps set the tone for your day. Whether it's starting your day with exercise, meditation, or planning your tasks, routines help automate decisions, conserve mental energy, and create a structure that supports your goals.

8. **Balancing Short-Term and Long-Term Goals**

It's easy to get caught up in daily tasks, but maintaining a balance between short-term and long-term goals is key to sustained success. While immediate tasks may feel urgent, ensuring that you're regularly working on long-term objectives will lead to meaningful progress over time. Regularly reviewing and reflecting on your goals helps ensure that your actions align with your broader vision.

9. **Staying Motivated and Avoiding Burnout**

Staying motivated is essential for long-term productivity. It's natural to lose motivation at times, but by setting clear goals, rewarding progress, and remembering your "why," you can reignite your drive. It's also critical to recognize the signs of burnout and take preventive measures such as scheduling breaks, practicing self-care, and setting realistic expectations.

10. **The Power of Reflection and Adaptation**

One of the most overlooked aspects of productivity is the power of reflection. Regularly reviewing your progress allows you to evaluate what's working, what's not, and where improvements can be made. Reflection also enables you to adapt your strategies as circumstances change. Whether it's tweaking your schedule, adjusting your goals, or trying new productivity techniques, staying flexible and evolving is key to sustained success.

Conclusion: Putting It All Together

The path to productivity is a journey, not a destination. By applying the principles discussed throughout this book—setting SMART goals, mastering time management, staying motivated, and embracing reflection—you can build a strong foundation for achieving your personal and professional objectives. Remember, productivity isn't about perfection; it's about consistent progress, self-improvement, and learning to work smarter, not harder.

As you move forward, keep these key points in mind. They will serve as your guide to staying focused, motivated, and productive in all areas of life. With the right mindset and strategies, you can unlock your full potential and create a more balanced, fulfilling, and successful life.

Your Roadmap to Mastery

Mastery is not a destination but a continuous journey. Whether you're striving to master a skill, improve your productivity, or achieve long-term personal and professional success, the process requires dedication, strategy, and a clear roadmap. The path to mastery is built on a solid foundation of habits, learning, reflection, and adaptation. This roadmap will guide you through the essential steps to achieving mastery in any area of your life, providing you with practical strategies to stay focused, motivated, and committed to your goals.

1. **Set Clear, Achievable Goals**

The first step on your journey to mastery is to define exactly what you want to achieve. Setting clear, achievable goals gives you direction and purpose. Without a clear goal, it's easy to get distracted or lose motivation. Use the SMART framework—Specific, Measurable, Achievable, Relevant, and Time-bound—to create goals that are concrete and attainable. Break larger goals into smaller milestones, allowing you to track progress and celebrate small wins along the way. This will keep you motivated and help you build momentum.

2. **Commit to Lifelong Learning**

Mastery requires continuous learning. No matter how skilled you become, there will always be more to learn. Commit to being a lifelong learner by constantly seeking new information, refining your techniques, and staying curious. Whether through books, courses, podcasts, or mentorship, make learning a regular part of your routine. The world is always evolving, and to stay ahead, you must evolve with it. Remember, even the most successful experts never stop learning—they view every challenge as an opportunity for growth.

3. **Develop Productive Habits**

Mastery isn't achieved through short bursts of effort but through consistent, daily practice. To make progress, you need to develop productive habits that support your goals. These habits should be specific and sustainable, integrated into your daily routine. For example, if you're trying to master a new language, dedicate 20-30 minutes each day to practice. Establish morning and evening routines that set the tone for your day and help you wind down effectively. Building productive habits takes time, but once they're established, they will work in the background, steadily moving you toward mastery.

4. **Practice Deliberately**

Deliberate practice is a key component of mastering any skill. It involves practicing with intention, focusing on areas that need improvement, and continuously challenging yourself. Rather than just going through the motions, deliberate practice requires effort, focus, and regular feedback. Set aside time for focused practice sessions where you push yourself outside your comfort zone, analyze your performance, and make adjustments. Over time, this targeted approach will lead to substantial improvements and deeper mastery.

5. **Embrace Failure as Feedback**

The road to mastery is rarely smooth, and setbacks are inevitable. However, it's important to shift your mindset from fearing failure to viewing it as feedback. Each failure is an opportunity to learn something valuable about yourself, your approach, or the task at hand. Instead of getting discouraged, ask yourself: "What can I learn from this?" Use each failure as a stepping stone toward mastery, refining your techniques and adapting your strategies. Resilience in the face of failure is what separates those who achieve mastery from those who give up early.

6. **Stay Disciplined and Consistent**

Discipline is the glue that holds your progress together. It's easy to stay motivated when things are going well, but true mastery requires discipline even during challenging times. Consistency is the secret weapon of high achievers. By showing up every day, regardless of how you feel, you slowly but surely make progress. Create a schedule or accountability system that ensures you're making consistent efforts, even when motivation wanes. Remember, small, consistent actions compound over time to create significant results.

7. **Reflect and Adjust Regularly**

Reflection is a critical step in the roadmap to mastery. It allows you to analyze your progress, identify areas for improvement, and adjust your strategies accordingly. Take time regularly—whether weekly, monthly, or quarterly—to review your goals and the progress you've made. What's working? What's not? What could you do differently? Reflection helps you stay aligned with your goals and ensures that you're constantly evolving in your approach. This process of continual improvement is what leads to mastery.

8. **Find Mentors and Build a Support Network**

Mastery is rarely achieved in isolation. Having mentors and a support network can accelerate your progress and keep you motivated. Seek out mentors who have already achieved mastery in the areas you're pursuing. Learn from their experiences, ask for advice, and model their habits and strategies. Additionally, surrounding yourself with like-minded individuals who are also on the path to mastery creates a sense of accountability and motivation. Engage in communities where you can share your journey, exchange ideas, and support each other's growth.

9. **Celebrate Progress, Not Perfection**

Mastery is a long-term pursuit, and along the way, it's crucial to celebrate your progress, no matter how small. Focusing solely on the end goal can be overwhelming, but recognizing and appreciating the incremental improvements you make will keep you motivated. Remember, mastery is not about perfection; it's about progress. Every step you take brings you closer to your goal, and each improvement, no matter how minor, is a victory worth celebrating.

Conclusion: Mastery is a Journey

Your roadmap to mastery is not a straight line—it's a dynamic process filled with learning, growth, and adaptation. By setting clear goals, committing to learning, developing productive habits, and embracing failure, you create the foundation for mastery. Stay disciplined, reflect on your progress, and adjust your strategies as needed. With the right mindset and persistence, mastery is within your reach. Remember, it's not about reaching the finish line but about the growth and transformation you experience along the way. Keep moving forward, and enjoy the journey of becoming a master in your chosen field.

Final Thoughts

As we wrap up this exploration of productivity, it's essential to reflect on everything you've learned and how it applies to your life. Productivity is not just about checking tasks off a list—it's about finding balance, purpose, and efficiency in the way you approach your goals. More than anything, it's about intentionality—knowing what matters to you and structuring your time, energy, and focus around that.

1. **The Importance of Personal Alignment**

One of the core ideas we've discussed is the importance of aligning your productivity with your personal values and goals. It's easy to get caught up in the busyness of everyday life, constantly moving from one task to another. But real productivity comes from ensuring that what you're working on brings you closer to your bigger goals and fulfills your deeper ambitions.

Take time to reflect on what truly matters to you. What are the areas of your life that you want to improve or focus on? Whether it's career growth, personal development, or spending more time with loved ones, ensuring that your productivity practices align with your values will not only make you more effective but also bring a greater sense of fulfillment.

2. **The Power of Small, Consistent Actions**

As you move forward, remember that productivity isn't about giant leaps, but about small, consistent actions. The biggest goals are often achieved through steady progress, not overwhelming bursts of effort. The strategies you've learned, like the Pomodoro Technique, time blocking, and prioritization methods, are all built around this principle.

Consistency is the foundation of long-term success. Whether you're trying to improve your health, career, or personal life, it's the little things you do daily that compound over time. This is why it's so crucial to stay disciplined and stick with the habits and systems that work for you.

3. **Embracing Flexibility and Adaptation**

While consistency is key, so is flexibility. Life is unpredictable, and no productivity system is perfect. There will be days when things don't go according to plan, and that's okay. What matters is your ability to adapt and adjust your approach as necessary.

You may need to revisit your goals and priorities regularly, especially as circumstances in your life change. Being too rigid can lead to frustration and burnout, but embracing flexibility allows you to stay productive even when things don't go as expected. Learn to adapt your strategies and give yourself permission to change course if needed.

4. **Avoiding Perfectionism**

Another significant lesson is to avoid perfectionism. The pursuit of perfection can often hold you back from getting things done. It can make you overthink, delay decisions, or spend too much time on tasks that don't require it. Accept that not everything needs to be perfect; sometimes, good enough is just that—good enough.

Progress matters more than perfection. Don't let the fear of making mistakes or producing less-than-perfect work stop you from moving forward. Each step you take, even if imperfect, is still progress toward your goals. In the end, it's the cumulative effect of those steps that leads to real achievement.

5. **Mindset Matters**

Productivity is as much about mindset as it is about tools and techniques. A positive, growth-oriented mindset can fuel your motivation, help you overcome setbacks, and keep you on track when things get tough. On the other hand, a negative or fixed mindset can be a major roadblock to progress.

Cultivating the right mindset involves being kind to yourself, staying resilient, and recognizing that every challenge is an opportunity to grow. You will face obstacles, but those who approach their challenges with a mindset of learning and growth tend to thrive in the long run.

6. **The Role of Reflection**

As you continue your productivity journey, never underestimate the power of reflection. Regularly reviewing your progress and adjusting your strategies can help you stay on the right track. Reflection gives you the space to celebrate your successes, learn from your mistakes, and realign with your goals when necessary.

Set aside time each week or month to reflect on what's working and what's not. This practice not only enhances your productivity but also increases self-awareness, allowing you to better understand your strengths and areas for improvement.

7. **Sustaining Motivation and Energy**

Productivity isn't just about managing your time—it's also about managing your energy. Burnout is real, and it can severely affect your ability to stay productive. To sustain your motivation and energy, it's essential to take breaks, recharge, and prioritize self-care.

Remember, productivity isn't about working harder but about working smarter. Taking care of your physical and mental well-being will ensure that you have the stamina to stay productive in the long run. Listen to your body, recognize when you need rest, and don't be afraid to take a step back when necessary.

8. **Celebrate Your Progress**

Lastly, don't forget to celebrate your progress. Recognizing your achievements, no matter how small, is essential for staying motivated. Productivity isn't just about getting more done—it's about moving toward a life that feels meaningful and satisfying to you.

As you move forward, take time to appreciate how far you've come. Whether it's checking off tasks, reaching milestones, or achieving long-term goals, every bit of progress deserves recognition. This will not only boost your morale but also remind you why you're on this journey in the first place.

Conclusion: Embrace the Journey

In conclusion, productivity is an ongoing journey, not a final destination. By adopting the right strategies, mindset, and habits, you can continuously improve your productivity while staying aligned with your personal goals. Remember to be patient with yourself, stay flexible, and enjoy the process. As you embrace these principles, you'll not only become more productive but also more fulfilled in every aspect of your life. Keep moving forward, and remember—the best is yet to come.

Resources

Recommended Books and Articles

The journey to improving productivity is never-ending, and having the right resources can make all the difference. Whether you're just beginning to explore productivity concepts or you're looking to refine your approach, a wealth of literature is available to guide you. Below are some highly recommended books and articles that delve deep into the science of productivity, time management, and personal development. These works are sure to provide valuable insights, practical tools, and inspiration to elevate your productivity game.

1. **"Atomic Habits" by James Clear**

Why Read It?

"Atomic Habits" is one of the most popular books on habit formation, offering practical strategies for making small changes that lead to big results. James Clear breaks down the science of how habits work and provides actionable steps for building good habits and breaking bad ones. If you're looking to increase your productivity, this book is essential because productivity isn't just about doing more—it's about doing the right things consistently. Clear's advice on habit stacking and creating systems for success can be directly applied to boost your daily output.

Key Takeaway:
Small, consistent actions lead to massive long-term success.

---

2. **"Deep Work: Rules for Focused Success in a Distracted World" by Cal Newport**

Why Read It?
In today's world of constant distractions, deep, focused work is becoming increasingly rare—and incredibly valuable. Cal Newport's "Deep Work" teaches readers how to cultivate the ability to focus without distractions, enabling them to produce high-quality work in less time. This book is particularly relevant for anyone struggling to manage interruptions and maintain focus, making it a must-read for boosting productivity.

Key Takeaway:
Learning how to enter a state of deep work can lead to profound improvements in both the quality and quantity of your output.

---

3. **"The 7 Habits of Highly Effective People" by Stephen R. Covey**

Why Read It?
A timeless classic, "The 7 Habits of Highly Effective People" provides a holistic approach to personal and professional effectiveness. Covey's principles focus on building strong foundational habits that lead to

long-term success. This book isn't just about time management—it's about managing your life in a way that aligns with your values and goals. Covey's concept of "beginning with the end in mind" is an essential mindset for anyone looking to be more productive and intentional with their time.

Key Takeaway:
Productivity is about aligning your daily actions with your long-term goals and values.

---

4. **"The Pomodoro Technique" by Francesco Cirillo**

Why Read It?
If you're interested in time management techniques, "The Pomodoro Technique" is a simple yet effective method that can dramatically improve your focus and productivity. The technique involves breaking your work into 25-minute intervals (called Pomodoros), followed by short breaks. Francesco Cirillo's book explains the philosophy behind the technique and provides tips for maximizing its effectiveness. It's an excellent tool for overcoming procrastination and managing your time more efficiently.

Key Takeaway:
Working in focused bursts with regular breaks can enhance concentration and reduce burnout.

---

5. **"Essentialism: The Disciplined Pursuit of Less" by Greg McKeown**

Why Read It?
In a world where we're often pressured to do more, Greg McKeown's "Essentialism" challenges readers to focus on doing less—but better. The book teaches the art of saying "no" to distractions and non-essential tasks, allowing you to focus only on the things that truly matter. This

minimalist approach to productivity helps you eliminate the clutter and busywork that often bogs you down, freeing up time and energy for more meaningful work.

Key Takeaway:
The key to true productivity is focusing on fewer tasks that have the greatest impact.

---

6. **"The One Thing" by Gary Keller and Jay Papasan**

Why Read It?
"The One Thing" emphasizes the importance of prioritization in productivity. The authors argue that by focusing on just one task—the most important one—you can achieve extraordinary results in less time. This book is perfect for anyone struggling with overwhelm or decision fatigue, offering a clear and straightforward strategy to help you streamline your to-do list and focus on what really matters.

Key Takeaway:
Focus on the single most important task each day to achieve better results in both the short and long term.

---

7. **Articles by Productivity Experts**

In addition to books, articles can be a quick way to gain productivity insights. Here are a few must-read articles by leading experts in the field:

- **"Why Procrastinators Procrastinate" by Tim Urban** (Wait But Why Blog):
This humorous yet insightful article dives into the psychology behind procrastination and provides a fresh perspective on how to overcome it.

- **"The Myth of Multitasking" by Christine Rosen** (The New Atlantis):

This article explores why multitasking is detrimental to productivity and offers a case for single-tasking as a more effective approach.

- **"The Eisenhower Matrix: How to Make Tough Decisions"** (James Clear's Blog):
This article explains the Eisenhower Matrix, a time-management tool that helps you prioritize tasks by urgency and importance.

---

8. **Productivity Blogs and Podcasts**

Aside from books and articles, there are several blogs and podcasts worth checking out:

- **James Clear's Blog**: Focused on habits and productivity.
- **Cal Newport's "Deep Questions" Podcast**: Delves into productivity and focus.
- **The Tim Ferriss Show**: Offers practical productivity tips and interviews with high achievers.

Conclusion: Your Next Step

Incorporating insights from these books and articles into your daily routine will give you a well-rounded approach to productivity. Each of these resources offers unique perspectives, practical strategies, and actionable tips to help you become more efficient and intentional in your work and life. Start with one or two that resonate most with your current challenges, and as you apply their lessons, you'll begin to see real improvements in how you manage your time, focus, and energy.

Productivity Tools and Apps

In today's fast-paced world, staying productive is more important than ever. Fortunately, we live in a digital age where countless tools and apps are designed to help us organize tasks, manage time, and stay focused. Whether you're juggling multiple projects, struggling with procrastination, or trying to make better use of your time, the right productivity tools can make all the difference. Below are some of the best productivity apps and tools available that can significantly enhance how you work and manage your life.

1. **Trello**

Why It's Great:
Trello is a highly visual project management tool based on the concept of boards, lists, and cards. It's perfect for individuals and teams who need a simple way to track tasks, projects, and goals. You can create different boards for each project, add lists to represent the stages of the project, and use cards for individual tasks.

Trello allows for seamless collaboration, as you can easily assign tasks to team members, set due dates, and attach files. With its drag-and-drop interface, you can see your entire workflow at a glance. The tool is highly customizable and integrates with other apps like Google Drive and Slack, making it a versatile option for many productivity needs.

Key Features:
- Easy drag-and-drop functionality
- Customizable boards for different projects
- Collaboration tools for teams
- Integration with other productivity tools

---

2. **Todoist**

Why It's Great:
Todoist is one of the best task management apps available. It's ideal for creating to-do lists, setting reminders, and organizing your daily tasks. With Todoist, you can break down large projects into smaller tasks,

prioritize them, and set deadlines. One of the app's most powerful features is its ability to let you create recurring tasks, which is perfect for habits or regular responsibilities.

Todoist's interface is clean and simple, making it a breeze to use. You can also categorize tasks with labels and filters, helping you focus on what's most important. With Karma, Todoist's built-in productivity tracker, you can even gamify your task completion to keep yourself motivated.

Key Features:
- Create and manage tasks easily
- Recurring tasks and deadlines
- Labels and filters for organization
- Productivity tracking with Todoist Karma

---

3. **Notion**

Why It's Great:
Notion is an all-in-one productivity tool that combines notes, tasks, databases, and wikis into one platform. Whether you need a place to jot down ideas, collaborate with team members, or track personal goals, Notion is versatile enough to handle it all.

Its unique approach allows users to create a system tailored to their needs. You can create pages and sub-pages for different projects, and inside those, you can add anything from text and images to tables and timelines. The level of customization is unmatched, and Notion's flexibility makes it popular among teams, freelancers, and personal productivity enthusiasts alike.

Key Features:
- All-in-one workspace for notes, tasks, and databases
- Highly customizable interface
- Real-time collaboration for teams
- Works across devices

---

4. **RescueTime**

Why It's Great:
RescueTime is a time management app that runs in the background and tracks how you spend your time on your devices. This tool provides insights into your habits, helping you understand where your time goes during the day. By categorizing websites and apps into productive and non-productive, RescueTime shows you how much time you're spending on distractions like social media or productive work like writing or research.

It also allows you to set goals for how much time you want to spend on different activities and will alert you when you're veering off track. This data-driven approach to time management is perfect for people who struggle to stay focused or want to make better use of their work hours.

Key Features:
- Automatic time tracking across devices
- Detailed reports on how you spend your time
- Set goals and get alerts for productivity
- Categorizes activities as productive or non-productive

---

5. **Forest**

Why It's Great:
Forest is a unique productivity app designed to help you stay focused while also supporting environmental causes. The app encourages you to put down your phone and focus on the task at hand by planting a virtual tree. As you stay focused, the tree grows, but if you leave the app to check social media or get distracted, the tree dies.

Over time, you can grow an entire forest, which not only serves as a visual representation of your productivity but also allows you to earn rewards. These rewards can be used to plant real trees through the app's partnership with tree-planting organizations. Forest gamifies focus and concentration, making it fun to stay on task.

Key Features:
- Grow virtual trees as you stay focused
- Earn rewards and plant real trees
- Gamified approach to productivity
- Visual representation of your focus over time

---

6. **Slack**

Why It's Great:
For teams working remotely or in-office, Slack is a communication tool that centralizes conversations and makes collaboration easy. It's an instant messaging platform with channels for different topics or teams, so everyone can stay organized and on the same page. You can integrate it with various other tools like Google Drive, Trello, and Zoom to streamline workflow.

Slack eliminates the need for long email threads and allows for real-time communication. You can set reminders, share files, and even use it for quick polls or surveys. If your work relies heavily on communication and teamwork, Slack is an indispensable tool.

Key Features:
- Organized communication channels
- Real-time collaboration and messaging
- Integration with other productivity apps
- File sharing and task management

---

7. **Google Calendar**

Why It's Great:

Google Calendar is a classic, but still one of the best tools for time management. It allows you to schedule meetings, set reminders, and block out time for focused work. One of the best features is its ability to share calendars with others, making it easier for teams and families to coordinate schedules. You can also integrate it with task management apps like Todoist or Trello to keep everything synced in one place.

With its intuitive interface, setting up meetings, recurring events, and even adding detailed notes or video conferencing links is quick and easy. For those who rely heavily on scheduling to stay productive, Google Calendar remains a go-to tool.

Key Features:
- Schedule and share events easily
- Integrates with other apps for seamless workflow
- Set reminders and block time for tasks
- Syncs across all devices

Conclusion

The right productivity tools and apps can dramatically improve your ability to manage tasks, time, and focus. Whether you prefer simple to-do lists or comprehensive all-in-one solutions, the tools mentioned above cater to a variety of needs. The key is to find the ones that fit your workflow and help you stay organized, motivated, and on top of your tasks.

Online Communities and Support

In today's interconnected world, online communities have become powerful resources for learning, sharing experiences, and getting support. Whether you're seeking advice on personal development, professional growth, or even just motivation, joining an online community can be incredibly beneficial. These communities offer more than just a space to connect—they provide a wealth of collective knowledge, real-time problem-solving, and emotional support from like-minded individuals.

Here's how online communities and support networks can play a critical role in your journey toward greater productivity, self-growth, and success.

1. **Shared Knowledge and Expertise**

One of the biggest benefits of online communities is the ability to tap into a vast pool of collective knowledge. Instead of learning everything through trial and error, you can learn from the experiences of others. Many communities are centered around specific topics, such as time management, productivity, or entrepreneurship, where experts share their insights, tips, and advice.

For example, platforms like Reddit or specialized forums have groups dedicated to productivity methods such as Getting Things Done (GTD), the Pomodoro Technique, or bullet journaling. Members post articles, recommend books, and share personal success stories or challenges they've faced. This can be a great way to discover new tools and strategies you might not have considered before.

Why It's Effective:
By participating in these discussions, you not only learn faster but also gain practical insights from others who have faced similar challenges. You can ask questions and get multiple perspectives, which can speed up your learning curve and improve your productivity in no time.

---

2. **Accountability and Motivation**

Staying productive often requires a certain level of accountability, and online communities provide the perfect environment for that. Many groups have features such as accountability threads or group challenges, where members set personal goals and report on their progress. Knowing that you'll need to update the group on your achievements (or lack thereof) provides extra motivation to stay on track.

Communities like these, especially those found on platforms such as Facebook groups, Slack channels, or Discord, often encourage participants to check in regularly with their goals. The simple act of writing down what you aim to accomplish and sharing it with others can have a significant impact on how committed you feel. When you're part of a group, the support from fellow members often helps push you to meet your goals, even when your motivation is low.

Why It's Effective:
The accountability that comes from reporting your progress publicly drives you to stay consistent. This makes online communities an ideal space for people who need that extra push to stick to their plans and achieve their goals.

---

3. **Emotional Support and Encouragement**

Beyond sharing knowledge, online communities offer a sense of emotional support, which is especially important when you're facing setbacks or struggling with motivation. In these communities, you'll find others who understand the ups and downs of striving for personal or professional growth. They can offer encouragement, advice, or even just a listening ear when things get tough.

Being part of a supportive community can reduce feelings of isolation, especially if you're working remotely or dealing with challenges on your own. When you're feeling stuck or discouraged, simply sharing your concerns with others who can relate often lightens the emotional burden. In return, offering support to others can also boost your own morale, creating a positive cycle of giving and receiving.

Why It's Effective:

Knowing you're not alone in your journey and having a network of people cheering you on can make a huge difference in maintaining a positive mindset, which is crucial for long-term productivity and success.

---

4. **Opportunities for Collaboration and Networking**

Online communities also serve as networking platforms, offering opportunities to collaborate with people from around the world. Whether you're looking for a partner on a project, feedback on your work, or just some fresh ideas, the people you meet in these groups can become valuable contacts in your professional or personal life.

For example, in a productivity-focused group, you might connect with someone who has expertise in a particular time-management technique you've been wanting to try. You might also find collaborators for business ventures, writing projects, or other creative endeavors. These interactions can not only help you reach your goals faster but also open doors to opportunities you wouldn't have found otherwise.

Why It's Effective:
Collaboration and networking are key for growth, and online communities provide a convenient platform to meet like-minded individuals, exchange ideas, and work together toward common goals.

---

5. **Real-Time Problem Solving**

One of the unique advantages of online communities is their ability to provide real-time feedback and problem-solving. If you're struggling with a particular challenge—whether it's finding a better way to manage your time, overcoming procrastination, or figuring out the best software to use—you can post a question in the community and receive responses almost immediately. Platforms like Reddit's r/productivity or specialized Slack channels are particularly helpful for this.

The quick turnaround on advice and suggestions can help you solve problems more efficiently than you would if you were working through the issue alone. Having access to a community of experienced individuals means you're more likely to find a solution that works for you, and often much faster.

Why It's Effective:
The ability to get immediate feedback can save you time, prevent frustration, and provide solutions you might not have considered. This real-time support helps keep your productivity moving forward without unnecessary delays.

Conclusion

In the digital age, online communities have become essential spaces for learning, growth, and support. By joining these communities, you gain access to shared knowledge, motivation, emotional encouragement, and real-time solutions, all of which contribute to better productivity. Whether you're looking for accountability, problem-solving, or new networking opportunities, online communities offer a wealth of resources to help you stay on track and continue improving.

Closing Note for "Mastering Productivity: Proven Strategies to Stay Focused and Achieve Your Goals"

As you reach the final pages of this book, I want to take a moment to acknowledge the journey you've embarked on. Mastering productivity isn't just about checking tasks off a list—it's about creating a life that aligns with your values, your passions, and your vision for the future.

The strategies, techniques, and insights shared here are meant to serve as a guide. They are the tools to help you reclaim your time, sharpen your focus, and elevate your success. But remember, true productivity is deeply personal. It's about discovering what works best for *you*—your rhythm, your goals, your dreams.

As you move forward, don't strive for perfection. Instead, aim for progress. Celebrate each small win, adapt when things don't go as planned, and always keep learning. Productivity isn't a destination—it's a continuous process of growth and improvement.

The power to achieve your dreams lies in your hands, and now you have the tools to make it happen. Stay consistent, stay focused, and most importantly, stay kind to yourself throughout this journey. Surround yourself with people and communities that uplift and support your vision.

Thank you for allowing this book to be a part of your path toward greater productivity and success. I hope it's been as enriching for you to read as it has been for me to write. Now, go out there and create the life you've always imagined. You've got this!

Wishing you all the success in the world.

With gratitude and determination,

Sagar Gurwani